2015 WORLD HEALING

2015 WORLD HEALING

Barbara Wolf and Margaret Anderson

authorHOUSE®

AuthorHouse™
1663 Liberty Drive
Bloomington, IN 47403
www.authorhouse.com
Phone: 1 (800) 839-8640

Published by AuthorHouse 06/17/2015

ISBN: 978-1-5049-1841-1 (sc)
ISBN: 978-1-5049-1840-4 (e)

Library of Congress Control Number: 2015909773

Print information available on the last page.

This book is printed on acid-free paper.

This book is dedicated to Barbara's husband
Jack and to the rest of the world.

ACKNOWLEDGEMENTS

Chief Golden Light Eagle, Lakota Nation.
Grandmother SilverStar, Cherokee/Lakota Nation.
Patricia Cota-Robles and musician son. Musical Rapture.
Carmen Balhestero, São Paulo, Brazil.
Hideo Nakazawa, Japan.
Annelies Kessler, Switzerland.
Eric Salvisberg and Do Spiegel, Southern France.
Dr. Luke Cua and Irene, California.
Mike and Ruth Ssembiro, Uganda.
Mary Carlin, Earth Society.
George Eggleston, Agnihotra.
Frank Nelson, Agnihotra.
Gentle Bear, Richard du Fort.
Robert Quicksilver.
Ben Davidson.
Hiroyoshi Kawagishi.
Mitsuru Ooba.
Marianne Trost.
Judy Moss.
Emma Kunz.

Foreword

We firmly believe in what we believe, and we realize you may not agree with everything we believe. Probably we would not agree with everything you agree with. But let us put aside our differences and let us be friends.

It's the world that matters. Mother Earth needs help and we are trying to give it to her. That is all that is expected.

CONTENTS

INTRODUCTION

This book has to do with healing. World Healing. You are part of this world as well as the animals and the birds and the trees and the flowers. Mother Earth is the world and we are all sitting on her. What can we do to make her happy and what can we do to stop making her unhappy?

This book begins with our journey to New York City to be a part of a Winter Solstice celebration. Why are we attending? It is the moment when the sun gives the shortest time of light for the year and begins climbing to the longest time of light for the year. On the other side of the earth, the sun is doing the opposite.

Why is the sun important for us and Mother Earth? Every second when the sun faces the earth, 65 billion solar neutrinos pass through every square centimeter that faces the sun. These neutrinos are tiny neutral ones, meaning, they have neither positive or negative energy. However, everything has a consciousness including neutrinos. Therefore, they can be programed. We can think of these billions of neutral neutrinos and turn them into the positive energy of LOVE. Wouldn't that be the best energy for Mother Earth and all living on her?

Love is associated with health. It has been stated that if 144,000 people concentrate on the same thing at the same time, what the people want can happen. We can't judge how many people are concentrating on neutrinos but we can contribute to positive, healthy energy by changing solar neutrinos to the positive energy of Love.

There is the Law of Cause and Effect. Everything must be counted. What you think must be counted. And so, let us all contribute positive healthy energies by turning neutrino energy to the positive.

CHAPTER 1

WINTER SOLSTICE ~
NEW YORK CITY

A note: First Barbara will write her journey to New York City, and then Margaret will write. Both journals are in Chapter 1.

From Barbara:

December 19, 2014, 7:30 a.m.:

To celebrate the Winter Solstice, today we take the train to New York City. We will be joining those welcoming the beginning of a 'long' sun and the birth of a new year. Paul Winter will be performing his 35th Annual Winter Solstice Celebration at the Cathedral of St. John the Divine and we will be at this celebration. Winter is known for his interest in the Natural world, and last year his winter solstice event at the cathedral focused on elephants becoming extinct because of demand for their ivory. This year he is focusing on the coqui, the tree frog, and he taped this frog's famous evening sound while visiting a few months ago Danny Rivera in Puerto Rico. Rivera is 'the national voice of Puerto Rico' who will join Paul Winter at the cathedral. Singers, bomba drummers, and dancers will also be at the cathedral.

When Margaret and I begin our train journey to New York City this morning to attend the solstice ceremony, I leave my winter boots behind. No snow is on the ground and the weather itself seems friendly with not much thought of rain or snow. I have decided to follow that intuition.

And yes! The entire trip from beginning to end is without rain or snow. A bit windy and a bit cold, but Margaret and I are prepared for that. We are wearing layers, yes, layers of clothes to keep us warm!

On the train we are seated on the right side ready to look out the window at a wonderful view of the Hudson River. But first, before seeing the river, we must pass Syracuse, Rome, Utica, Amsterdam, Schenectady, etc. When we do cross the river, we watch the Hudson until we reach New York City.

Of course the first thing we check is the condition of the river in relationship to the algae that was increasing and increasing last spring when we took the train. But today, December 19, we see no algae! NONE.

WONDERFUL.

We do not see ducks or seagulls, but that is to be expected because the killing of the algae would come from adding poison to the water. My thought is that eventually the water will be safe enough for the ducks and seagulls to return.

When we reach Penn Station in New York City, the beginning of the evening dark has not yet started. Good. We will take the Number 2 express metro to 96th Street and then walk only two blocks to our hotel where we will spend three nights. Just around the corner is the Manhattan Diner, a wonderful place to eat when we are hungry.

December 20:

Last night's sleep held a lesson we did not realize would be a lesson. Yesterday when we entered our room, it was cold. A bright button on the heater told us the temperature was 59 degrees Fahrenheit. When we tried to set the temperature higher, the bright button remained at 59 degrees.

We phoned the front desk and a man came with an iron radiator to bring big heat into the room. And yes, it did bring big heat. Too much. There was no way to regulate this radiator, and so, when the room became hot, we turned it off. Then we began to notice a distracting strange noise, like clothes being washed. We phoned the front desk again and we learned that this noise came from steam passing through pipes. Well, there was nothing we could do about that!

The next morning, when we asked others to explain about steam traveling through pipes, we began to realize that this old brick hotel is probably connected to an old apartment complex with a common heating system. Water as steam was still being washed throughout these old buildings as well as the hotel.

Since water has a consciousness and will attempt to fit itself into a perfect, crystalline hexagram if it is fed the energies of love, we realize that if the energies of love are sent to the water, these love energies will be spread throughout the whole complex.

And so, instead of vowing never to return again to this hotel, tonight we will be ready when we hear the strange noise that sounds like clothes being washed in a washing machine. We will energize the noise with love. That will be our gift.

And yes, both of us sleep very well throughout the night!

December 20, we take the metro toward the Cathedral of St. John the Divine. When we exit the metro, we soon see the cathedral looming before us. We stop to look at the top far end of the building, home of the statue of Archangel Gabriel with his horn. Even though we cannot see it, we know that nearly below him is a stained glass window with a figure of the red-robed Christ.

At the steps of the cathedral, we join others waiting for the doors to open. A woman tells us she is from Brooklyn, and we tell her we will tomorrow be in Brooklyn to join gospel singers at the famous tabernacle.

When the cathedral doors open, we ticket holders go directly to our assigned seats. Ours are in the nave, and directly behind us, up a bit, is the stained glass window of the red-robed Christ. When we are seated, Margaret tells me to listen to the sound of the coqui frogs beeping. Amazing!

As we listen, we watch the cathedral seats fill and I think maybe 2,000 are here. Many seem accustomed to being here. They know what they are about to witness and they are ready!

At 2 p.m., Theresa Thomason, Paul Winter's vocalist, begins the program with a powerful, lusty voice. Does she always sing so powerfully? One cannot help but listen for a slip. Well, there is no slip. Theresa Thomason is FANTASTIC!

Now we watch Paul Winter and Danny Rivera performing together, singing together. They seem to be about the same age and their physiques are similar. One can nearly mistake them as being brothers.

A remarkable performance is when a gong master is hoisted above our heads to slowly move toward the stained glass window of the red-robed Christ figure behind us. Several times the movement stops and musicians give out POWERFUL HARSH SOUNDS. My theory is that this method weakens dark energies. Paul Winter has used a similar sound method at an earlier solstice we attended.

When the gong master reaches the stained glass window, the lights in the cathedral are FULL ON -- BRIGHT. And so, the sun has been brought home and this is the celebration of the birth of a new year.

Yes, Paul Winter's solstice performance has been an emotional moment for all of us watching.

December 21, Sunday:

Margaret and I cannot leave New York City without listening to the gospel singers at the Brooklyn Tabernacle. We take the Number 2 express metro from 96th Street and we whizz along with few stops. Soon we are in Brooklyn at Hoyt and we are getting off the train to walk up stairs. Now we must ask a ticket woman which way we walk to reach the tabernacle. Last spring I took the metro and Margaret was not with me, but now she is saying that she has investigated how to walk and my way is wrong. Well, what can one do? We usually have opposite opinions about which way to walk. Half the time she is right and half the time I am right.

The metro ticket woman tells us to walk up to street level, and then she gives us confusing directions. Never mind. There are plenty of people on the street who know the location of the Brooklyn Tabernacle. We walk along, and yes, we do reach the entrance. The doors are wide open, people are entering, and one glance inside tells me this is exactly where we should be.

A volunteer with today's colorful program in his hands greets us and leads us into a very large auditorium where he seats us so that nearly everyone entering the auditorium will walk by us. We soon discover they want to stop to shake hands. Friendly. They are very friendly.

We look at the brochure given to us and we see there are many announcements. Free admission to a White Christmas program that runs four days. A special candlelight prayer meeting. Married couples weekend getaway. Holiday concert with Tabernacle singers. Pastor Cymbala's new book, "Storm". A week of Prayer, etc., etc., etc.

Now, on the stage, a pastor is urging us to stand and sing. Soon we are boisterously singing and singing and singing. The words are displayed on a small TV screen hanging close to us. Some in the audience are raising their arms and hands. Others have their hands in prayer. All are boisterously singing.

Hearts are open, pouring out love.

To me, it does not matter what religion one prefers, or, maybe no religion. The singing will appeal to everyone. When the program is over, we are reluctant to leave.

In the afternoon we return to the Cathedral of St. John the Divine to listen to a performance called Dutch Christmas, typically celebrated 400 years ago at the time of Rembrandt. Music will be played and sung in the ancient Dutch language.

We are on the waiting list for this performance, and when we enter the cathedral, we check to see that our names are on the waiting list. Yes. Just before the performance is ready to begin, we are given two vacant seats.

The audience is quiet as we wait for the performers to enter the room, and I realize most around me have attended before. They are acutely aware of what they will begin to hear.

As for myself, I have never listened to ancient Dutch music and it is a surprise to me when they begin singing in precise, patterned tones. They are the exact opposite of what the Puerto Ricans had given us yesterday at the cathedral -- raucous, spontaneous tones from their wide-open hearts.

Also, this music is the opposite of Brooklyn Tabernacle singing coming from wide-open hearts of Love. The ancient Dutch music is coming forth from minds concentrating on an exact pattern formed hundreds of years ago. It is as if nothing has changed over the centuries.

And so I have heard three different types of music here in New York City --traditional Christmas songs of today, Puerto Rican lively music, old Dutch singing of carefully patterned music.

To my surprise, this evening I will be hearing more music -- Puerto Rican singing. Our friend Gentle Bear takes us to a restaurant overlooking the Atlantic, and this restaurant is owned by his Puerto Rican friend. It is called the Don Coqui Restaurant, meaning the Tree-Frog Restaurant! How amazing that we should be hearing tree-frog sounds in the cathedral and then eat at a restaurant with the same name.

We sit overlooking the water, and we watch many Puerto Ricans having a wonderful, raucous time eating at tables around us. Their music is playing LOUDLY, ZESTFULLY and all are singing LOUDLY, ZESTFULLY. Even we three at our table are singing LOUDLY, ZESTFULLY.

What fun!

The restaurant owner gives us free hors d'oeuvres in honor of us coming to his restaurant after hearing the tree-frogs at the cathedral.

December 22, the day we say good-bye to our room and its hissing steam noise, we take the metro to Penn Station that is stuffed with people, many carrying wrapped presents. Obviously, they are on their way by train to celebrate Christmas somewhere. We line up with them and board an Amtrak train which, to our disappointment, is already so full we must take seats on the side of the train that will not ride along the Hudson River. We will be looking at new scenery.

Well, the scenery may be new to us, but not new to those living on this side of the tracks. Awful, discarded machinery, trucks, cars, etc. Abandoned, old houses. I keep thinking that New York State should begin a campaign to clean up these rubbish heaps going on and on and on.

We move along smartly and my thought is that we will have a better chance of arriving on time if we do move along smartly. Amtrak passengers are often at the mercy of freight trains. We must sit while long, loaded freight trains whizz past us 'a million miles an hour'!

Today, before reaching Utica, we stop and we wait and we wait and we wait, first for one freight train to approach and whiz by us and then we wait for another freight train that hasn't yet reached us. Finally it becomes dark, and then very dark. Our conductor apologizes from time to time.

And now he says an Amtrak train from Toronto to New York City has broken down and we must tow it to Rochester. It will take time to arrange the two trains for towing, he tells us.

And so we are stopped on a middle track with huge, loaded freight trains whizzing on both sides of us going 'a million miles an hour'. Eventually we are hooked onto the broken train and slowly we move along. An eight-hour train ride has turned into a twelve-hour train ride.

It is interesting that the passengers around us are patient. There is no yelling, no complaining. Is Christmas cheer holding up, or has patience taken over?

Now I need to stop and let Margaret tell you about her trip to New York City.

From Margaret:

December 19, 2014, I am up early Friday morning excited to go to New York City for the Winter Solstice celebration. When Joan Lenhard, our taxi driver, arrives at 7:30 a.m., I walk carefully out of the house mindful of my earlier experiences with ice. Barbara, who is used to Great Lakes weather, walks out without concern. For me it is very cold, 23 degrees, and there is thin, icy snow falling. The sky is grey.

At the train station, there is hardly room to sit, and we learn that our 8:26 a.m. train to New York City is sold out. Many students are going home and older couples are traveling for the holidays. When our train arrives, a kind conductor helps us board and we find seats on the right side that will face the Hudson River.

We go along for a time before reaching the river, and when we do, the sun comes out in full glory. In my mind, it becomes the *River of the Sun.* I send powerful, healing neutrinos changed to love to all the people of New York and the world. I see a magnificent sky with lenticular-like clouds dancing in front of the brilliant sun of high intensity. As I look at the sun directly, it begins to spin red, gold and green flashing light. I am thinking that all the people, all races, all nationalities, are Divine Beings.

When we reach New York City and pull into Penn Station, it is very crowded because it is rush hour. We leave the train to take an express subway to 96 Street where our hotel is located. This hotel is close to the Cathedral of Saint John the Divine where the Winter Solstice celebration will take place. We have dinner around the corner at the Manhattan Diner, where we always enjoy their food.

In the evening I write up my notes. To me, New Yorkers always feel intense. Now they feel even more intense. All traditions, all nationalities merge into one grand sandwich called New York City.

December 20, Saturday:

It is hard sleeping because of excessive noise coming from steam heat in the room. A crescendo of steam every three minutes. Quiet at first, then continuously louder. Then LOUD. Why are we suffering at a time when we need rest?

I ask the Dolphins to comment and they say:

We feel your discomfort and also your anticipation for the big Solstice event. The Sun welcomed you yesterday on your way to New York City.

The steam of heated water brings comfort to humans living in the old brick buildings of New York City. Steam delivering heat, steam delivering comfort for the residents is the energy of Love.

When Love is expressed, it makes perfect hexagons of water which, when turned to steam, releases comfort and compassion. Compassion, care, gratitude delivered against the icy cold of New York City.

The old city works in its old ways. New buildings, new delivery systems, old buildings, old delivery systems.

Can you understand the analogy and apply it to today's work? The steam brings comfort in the form of heat. The stream is generated by great boilers. Love is generated by compassionate hearts sending the warmth of Love to the human world, to the Nature world.

The Sun gives warmth, Love and Light for growing and sustaining life on the planet. Humans receive this Light and pass it on as Love to one another, to nurture each other. You can make the difference. You can add Love to Nature and you can add the frequency of nurture. Then all the planet will thrive. Love is never ending. Love is always expanding. Love is the essence of Life. Love is natural, a basic ingredient. All things grow with Love.

Everything has a consciousness. Even the smallest unit has a consciousness. Each unit responds to Love. Sunlight comes to the planet and the people respond in gratitude by giving Love. When the basic exchange is Love, then all things grow and thrive and live in harmony and balance.

This is our Winter Solstice message on the day of the shortest Light and the longest night. The day the Light returns. The day when Love is enhanced.

New York City is built on granite, tough volcanic rock. The River of Light flows through it. The granite holds the fire of Mother Earth, the basic core of Love. Every molecule, every atom, every smallest particle holds the Love intent of Mother Earth.

Today is the concert of Paul Winter celebrating the Winter Solstice and the return of the Light. The basic celebration is the Love of Mother Earth who gives home to all life forms on her surface (land, water, air).

All Nature knows the rhythm of the seasons reflecting the position of Mother Earth in relationship to the Sun. Stop today and acknowledge this wondrous planetary event. Cosmic event.

Stand with the little molecules that make up a great mountain or ocean or cloud or rainbow. All hold the imprint of Love and Light. In the awareness, there is Peace, Love and Light.

Spread this frequency throughout the planet. It is a grand special day to be in New York City to spread this intent of Peace, Love and Light through the planet, the planets, the universes.

This is our Dolphin message from space.

P.S. When you are at the cathedral, listen to the tree frogs. They announce the heartbeat of Mother Earth.

Close to noon, we walk to the Cathedral of Saint John the Divine to join a crowd beginning to form at the door. We stand with them, talking with them, waiting for the door to open.

At 1:00 p.m. we are allowed in and we begin following directions to our reserved seats. When we find them, a great organ is to our left and the red-robed Christ is high behind us in a stained glass window. Ahead of us is a large stage where the Solstice event will begin.

2:00 p.m., the performance starts with the church dark and the two musicians, Paul Winter and Danny Rivera, meeting each other warmly on stage. We see they have become close friends. Paul Winter begins playing his alto saxophone in his unique, melodic, mystical way. His presence is natural, calm, whereas when Danny Rivera begins singing and dancing, he is fiery with a Latin presence. Despite the differences, the two are very compatible.

As the program continues, the music becomes dissonant, expressing darkness on the Earth. A great golden brass sun gong begins rising and moving toward the window with the Christ wearing a red robe. The gong is struck again and again, crashing, splintering the darkness to bring back the Light. The darkness of the cathedral begins to fade, and when the gong reaches the window, the cathedral is LIGHT.

During the rising of the sun gong, I have been holding on my lap Vortexes that represent powerful energy fields from Higher Worlds.

*See Glossary for Vortex information.

The music continues on center stage and Danny Rivera announces, "We are all children of the same Sun". As the program continues, we hear beautiful singing of modern spirituals and we watch amazing dancing of African and Puerto Rican traditions. Then Paul Winter's daughter or granddaughter dances in a Celtic tradition.

A tribute is given to Pete Seeger and we listen to a recording of him singing "Ode to Pete". At the final end of the evening's performance is the Wolf Song, and the audience begins howling, calling the wolves, calling Nature, paying tribute to Nature. A fantastic event!

December 21, Sunday:

The morning is grey and cold as we arrive at the Brooklyn Tabernacle. When we enter the big doors, we feel warmth and we see a large Christmas tree full of lights. Yes, there is a great feeling of warmth here. Warmth of Spirit, warmth of presence, warmth of love vibration.

We move into the main sanctuary and see a sweep of rows of seats going down to the stage. We are fifteen minutes early, and when we are seated, we listen to singers on stage rehearsing. They are wearing red, green and white sweaters. As they are practicing, everyone entering the auditorium is welcoming everyone. The place abounds with love.

The service begins at 9:00 a.m. with singing and no written program. We stand and sing and sing. Words of the songs appear on large and small screens near us and so we have no difficulty singing with the others. These are Christmas songs intermingled with praise songs. I feel this place is a New York Spiritual Electrical Power Station sending out love and light vibration to the city, to the world.

Before giving us a beautiful sermon, the minister asks first-time visitors to stand up to be acknowledged. Then he tells us about a special Christmas event for the homeless and the needy. He says nearly 2,000 were fed by 400 volunteers. Trucks came to deliver toys given to all the children. Hearing this, I begin to cry and the man beside me cries. All in the tabernacle are moved. When I return to my computer a few days later, I search for Brooklyn Tabernacle singing and I find it. My heart soars from the memories of being there.

This afternoon we return to the Cathedral of Saint John The Divine to attend "A Dutch Christmas", a singing performance by a group called Early Music New York. They will sing Dutch Renaissance music with harmonies and melodies from the 17th Century and earlier. I listen to this beautiful melodious music, a celebration of a time past. My mind loves it. It is a jewel in a jewel case.

Within two days, we have listened to three musical performances, all different -- Paul Winter of the Light, Brooklyn Tabernacle of Love, and Dutch Renaissance Music of precise Sound and Harmony.

Tonight we will return to thoughts of the Winter Solstice when Gentle Bear picks us up in his spacious white truck and takes us to Don Coqui Restaurant, a restaurant of celebrations. Joyful families are gathered, singing, dancing, enjoying delicious food. It is interesting that the name of this restaurant reflects the name of the Puerto Rican tree frog honored at the Winter Solstice celebration at the cathedral.

Tonight, the exact moment of the Winter Solstice arrives at 6:03 p.m. and we are seated at a large window by the water of Long Island Sound. I spread out the Vortexes and the new earth calendar given to the world by the Native Americans. They call this The EarthStar Way Calendar. For them, today is the first day of the new calendar year. The combination of these two events is amazing -- the beginning of the new calendar year and the exact moment of the Winter Solstice.

*See Glossary for Vortex details and calendar information in the Vortexes section.

Our friend Gentle Bear tells us wonderful stories of the area as we are having a delightful dinner. This is a perfect closure to our trip.

December 22, Monday:

With our suitcases in hand we go to Penn Station to return home by train. Along the way, as the sun sets, we receive a sun blessing as it bursts though the clouds.

CHAPTER 2

WEATHER

From Barbara:

Something seems to have gone wrong with the weather. Has it gone crazy or are our thoughts too extreme?

Last summer felt like springtime. Where was the heat? September seemed comfortable because it felt warmer than the usual fall weather. What is happening? In November we needed to go to Colorado to speak at a conference. When we checked the Internet for temperature predictions in Colorado, we learned that a Polar Vortex was beginning to make its way south from northern Canada.

Polar Vortex? What is that? To learn more, we need to wait until we return from Colorado. But, as a precaution, we will take our boots with us.

And yes, we needed them, plus warm winter clothes. While we were there, we didn't see a thermometer but we were told it was below zero (Fahrenheit). In mid November?

When we returned to the Northeast, Buffalo was on the verge of experiencing a seven-foot plus snowfall, one foot after the other! Whoever heard of such a thing? Our destination was only seventy miles east of Buffalo and we did not want THAT reaching us!

Now we begin receiving announcements that a Polar Vortex is heavily influencing weather. The South is receiving Arctic cold at the wrong time of the year. What is happening?

Well, Polar means Arctic which to me means that last November a Polar Vortex did not stop coming south from the Arctic until it reached the southern part of the North American Continent. It was so large, it spread coast-to-coast thousands of miles. A lot of my life has been lived in the northern part of the American Continent and no one ever spoke about a Polar Vortex.

Apparently, another item called the jet stream had a great deal to do with the Polar Vortex abnormality going so far south. The jet stream is a flow of air that influences the Polar Vortex. When the jet stream is abnormal, the Arctic is warm because the jet stream has pushed the cold south rather than remaining in the north.

Now Margaret will give you channeling so you are able to read about weather from both of us.

———————————

Margaret Channeling:

Dear Yolanda of the Pleiades, can you comment on the weather patterns? The Arctic Polar Vortex has moved south making the Great Lakes cold like Alaska. When I was growing up in the Washington, D.C. area, I did not remember extremes in the weather except for a hurricane or two that would come up the East Coast bringing high winds, rains, and tides.

What is happening to the weather now? It seems overwhelming.

Yolanda: In the old days there were still tornadoes in Oklahoma and Missouri and great drought in the Southwest -- California and Texas. But now things have speeded up. Mother Earth's interior rotation has speeded up. The earth is crystalline based and not magnetic. Things move more quickly. Time has speeded up. There are now many more people living on Mother Earth than earlier.

And earlier there was much more uncultivated land in the United States, Brazil, Canada, and elsewhere. Vast stands of trees helped moderate and balance the weather. Now there are cement parking lots and roadways where there were once fields and forests. Earlier rains could be absorbed into the land and now rains go running off the land as they would go off roofs.

The weather and wind and jet currents are affected by human agitation. Storms within the minds of individuals easily can make a collective mass of agitation. Mass fear. Mass shock. Mass sadness can affect the atmosphere. All are related.

Heavy pollution now in the air, especially around cities, has affected the air, the storms. Cities affect their own climates.

Parks, forests, beaches calm individuals. Music, art, crystals, all add to calming the environment. Look to the weather as a joy for each day. What a gift to live on a planet that is a perfect balance of air, land and water. When things go out of balance, is this man made?

Honor your life. Be sure to be grateful and speak your gratefulness in your heart. Agendas belong to the mind. Calmness, gratitude, compassion come from the heart.

Give calmness to the weather. Give gratitude to the rain, the snow. Give thanks to the wind that brings fresh air to your doorstep. It is all quite amazing. You are in your own 'land rover' – your body – exploring this amazing planet with a mission to make this place a better place. A place to be cherished, honored, the way the original peoples did. 21st Century humanity needs to open its receptors to Mother Earth's condition and needs. If humanity continues to live in a shut-down mode, closing its eyes to problems, then quickly these problems will come crashing on doorsteps. Then humanity will wake up and see how fragile its living space really is.

Will there be more earthquakes in Dallas and Washington, D.C.? Will there be seven-foot snowdrifts in your backyard? Will the ocean flood the subways of New York City? On and on. It will be the same in every part of the world.

Wake up. Be conscious of your actions! Do not do 'malpractice' practices that will hurt Mother Earth and her life forms -- tearing up vegetation and trees at the waterfronts, paving open land with developments and malls, grazing lands becoming deserts.

Look to the old ways of the early people. They have the wisdom of the land. They can talk to the plants and get wisdom. You will go forward by going backwards in learning and understanding.

We are with you.

With love, Yolanda of the Pleiades

From Barbara:

When Buffalo was hit by a big snowstorm refusing to stop, we kept our minds on blue sky and sunshine. We played the music called Musical Rapture.

*See Glossary for Musical Rapture.

Not for a moment did we keep our minds on the storm coming to us even though we knew it would be normal for us to be the next in line. Well, it came marching from northwest, but, without stopping, it went south of us. We even learned that people watched it moving south of us. Thank you, Polar Vortex storm, for bypassing us!

CHAPTER 3

PACIFIC PLATE
MOVEMENTS ~ JAPAN

W e need to write you about a world increase in volcanoes and earthquakes. More and more seem to be happening every day. We are not experts on this, but we need to tell you anyway, and we will begin with Japan.

A few years ago when we were there, we visited Sakurajima, the most active volcano in Japan, and maybe the most active in the world. Via Margaret channeling, we asked Sukurajima what is happening and here is the answer:

Because of changes in earth's magnetism and gravity, this affects the lava within the earth. It becomes more buoyant, more active, not as compressed. This is also in line with the solar activity and change in the sun's nature.

Everything is more active – weather conditions, earthquakes, volcanoes, storms, wind weather patterns, etc.

Humanity seems to become more tense and anxious. Differences between groups more irritating; the political rhetoric harsh. Violence, violent actions are broadcast around the world causing instability in the minds of people. This affects the environment.

Calmness and Unity can break up and smooth over fractured frequencies. Calmness in Self and Unity between peoples. Face as one the deep snowstorms, the wind and rainstorms, and then the uneven climate may lessen in its extremes.

We ask ourselves what can we do to help? We are world healers. We can give peace and love. In a split second, anyone can give peace and love to all living on Mother Earth. It is matter of THOUGHT. Give Peace and Love to the entire all of Mother Earth's surface, and it is done. Of course it won't stick to many because it is not their habit to accept peace. Never mind. One does one's best.

And now, unexpectedly, in a split second, Mother Earth sends Barbara a thought that she is pleased we are giving peace to folks living on her. Thank you, Mother Earth!

We begin playing cosmic music called Paneurhythmy, and with our minds, we visualize that this music can help ease Mother Earth's quake problem in the Pacific. This cosmic music is a handy tool for us.

* See Glossary for Paneurhythmy music.

We need to explain more to you about why we worry about Japan. This country is not only at the mercy of the Pacific Plate and the Philippine Plate but two other plates are involved – the North American Plate and the Eurasian Plate. When plates move and lock or unlock if the stress is too great, Japan will feel shaking of the land when these events happen.

Again, plate activity means that earlier movement has locked plates together. This locking builds stress. Stress relief comes with breakage called an earthquake. The bigger the stress, the bigger the breakup, bigger earthquakes.

Scientists warn that Japan is due for another 8 point plus earthquake which caused a catastrophe at the Fukushima nuclear power plant in 2011. That was a 9 point. Our job is world healing. We want no more Fukushima incidents. We will do our best to help avert this.

A couple months ago, when the Pacific Plate facing Fukushima had two 4 point earthquakes almost in line with each other, we asked the Higher Worlds why there were two 4 point earthquakes when scientists were talking about an 8 point earthquake. We were told that these two 4 point earthquakes were not as damaging as one 8 point. Our thought is that the scientists 'got what they were talking about'.

Incidentally, Mother Earth is making new land from one of her earth rumblings and so you can understand that not only is there destruction but also creativity behind the shaking of the land.

As for Japan today, the active volcano Sakurajima is close to the city called Kagoshima. A few years ago we stayed overnight in Kagoshima and we worried about the folks in that city. How can their lungs take volcanic ash and steam given to them by Sakurajima eruptions? We feel the people should leave.

Are they leaving? No, but we would leave.

Now, we learn from the Internet, that earth activity in Vanuatu, a series of islands not close to Japan, can actually help trigger big earthquakes in Japan. In 2011,Vanuatu was a flag for the Fukushima earthquake disaster. Now, February 2015, we learn a large earthquake has just occurred on Vanuatu. Are we to ignore the possibility of a large earthquake ready to happen in Japan?

Now that we understand that earthquakes are caused by plates releasing stress when there is too much buildup, shouldn't we try to lessen the stress of plates throughout the entire area? This would entail thousands of miles, although, when one uses the mind, mileage does not matter.

We need help. Who can help us? We decide to call in the Aborigines of Australia. A few years ago, Barbara worked esoterically with them throughout the world, and they were very cooperative.

And so, in meditation today, we ask them for help. We ask them to ease stress by using their didgeridoo instruments 'to sound' the plates. Less stress would mean no large earthquakes.

Yes, the Aborigines agree to help us! WONDERFUL!

They begin playing their music with their didgeridoos, and we begin playing cosmic music as we go into meditation to ease the plate problem.

*See Glossary for Australian Aboriginal music.

What fun!

As a footnote, while we are writing you, there have been no large destructive earthquakes in Japan.

Margaret Channeling:

I ask Emma, can you comment on us calling in the Aborigines to place the energies of the didgeridoo sound on the Pacific plate system to help steady the plates?

From Emma:

Mother Earth feels the Aborigine music directly in her heart! The music of the wood tube resonates with the plate structure of her being.

The didgeridoo goes between all elements – fire, lava, land, air, water – linking the hearts of all those listening.

The music says wake up. Mother Earth is alive and well!! Wake up animals, birds, sea creatures, humans, kangaroos, on and on through all Kingdoms.

The plates pause when the music is heard. Plates move softly in the presence of the didgeridoo.

The force, the power of the music enhances Mother Earth's power and being-ness. All things come to unity in the presence of the didgeridoo.

Stop, listen, watch. Proceed softly in the presence of the Aborigine didgeridoo music.

A success!!

You had the plates' attention – all working together.

With love,
Emma

*See Glossary: Emma Kunz.

Sakurajima has more to say when Margaret writes a mental letter to him saying we love him and we have always loved his balance and closeness to the human world.

He comments.

Dear Margaret. Yes, I am balanced and close to the people, and yet I am an outlet for pressure building up inside Mother Earth. I am a powerful volcano that is a release valve for Mother Earth. The fire inside is powerful and dynamic. The people need to be aware of the pressures of the volcanoes, internal and external within Mother Earth and beyond Mother Earth – the sun, the planets, cosmic forces.

Pressure builds. The fire moves to the surface and discharges. That is how the land is formed. That is the Creation of Nature of Mother Earth. That which was inside is now outside, through a buildup of powerful force.

I am different now. My job is to release pressure for the Earth. The human neighbors need to take this into account. Life is different now. Everything has ramped up 1,000 fold. More and More. Be aware. Living within a close proximity of a volcano is living with fire as a neighbor.

I am for the whole of the planet. I am global, not local. Widen your view of me and other aspects of Mother Earth and the Solar System. Wake up. Things are as they are. I accept your love and your light as my people give me as well.

But I am a force of Nature in my Being. Mother Earth is alive and well. Living. Breathing. Expanding. Exploding. Loving. All in One.

Sakurajima.

May 17, we have been intending to be in Japan to participate in the inauguration of The Fuji Declaration which the world is being asked to support and will support. It has to do with Peace.

* See Glossary: The Fuji Declaration.

Today there is great crisis and unrest throughout the world and this needs to be changed so peace can reign and well-being will be for all. The ceremony will be at the foot of Mount Fuji to help bring forth the Divine Spark that is in all our hearts.

However, we have cancelled. Mother Earth unrest has brought caution.

Here is the background. Near Mount Fuji is another volcano called Mount Hakone. This is one of 110 in Japan. People like to come to Mount Hakone to bathe in hot springs and climb to the top of the mountain. In May, people tend to relax and go to places like hot springs. Because Mount Hakone is close to Mount Fuji, many are expected to go in May at the time of The Fuji Declaration.

However, the authorities have just closed this area because of increased steam coming from Mount Hakone. Is Mother Earth trying to tell us that she is ready for another eruption? Only last September she unexpectedly blew her top at another volcano while people were climbing. Many died.

Margaret and I do not have experience living in volcanic areas and so caution presides with us. We will stay away. By the way, we have written a separate chapter for The Fuji Declaration. It is Chapter 11.

_____

CHAPTER 4

MORE PACIFIC OCEAN PLATE MOVEMENTS

W e need to write you more about plate movements in the Pacific area. A 5.2 undersea earthquake has sparked our interest in the Juan de Fuca Plate.

In particular, why should we be interested in this plate? Is it located near Japan? No, far away. Across the ocean, in the water about fifty miles west of Vancouver Island, North American Continent. This area is called the Cascadia Subduction Zone and this subduction zone is between the North American Plate and the Pacific Plate. Two other plates, the Explorer Plate and the South Gorda Plate, run with the Juan de Fuca Plate.

Large parts of the Juan de Fuca Plate have locked together as the plate is being forced under the North American Plate. We explained earlier that this locking builds stress, and stress relief comes from breakage called earthquake. The bigger the stress, the bigger the earthquake. A 5.2 earthquake is considered big here.

The average time for a mega quake, a name for the world's largest earthquakes, is between 8 to 240 years here. The last one was over 300 years ago, and that mega quake was estimated to be 9 on the Richter scale.

We learn that a movie on earthquakes is coming to the public this year. Why is this happening? Why are the people being shown something causing panic? And then we think maybe this movie is actually a blessing in disguise. It will alert people to prepare for an unexpected emergency.

We remember the theory of the hundredth monkey. When something is taught and one hundred learn, this teaching will spread to all. With this in mind, we realize that yes, the movie could be a blessing in disguise because of the great number seeing it.

A check of the Internet shows that a number of volcanoes are located in the Juan de Fuca area. One of them, Mount Saint Helens, erupted violently in 1980, causing tremendous destruction. Now that the Juan de Fuca Plate has moved enough to cause our attention, and it is opposite Mount Saint Helens, could we be waiting for more disruption?

From Barbara:

I remember the need to stop a big shifting of plates in Siberia a few years ago. My mind showed me many dead people floating down a huge tsunami-made river caused by the big shifting of plates in the Pacific. However, I helped stop the shifting of plates and the deaths did not occur. When I channeled why the deaths were shown when they did not happen, I was told by the Higher Worlds that if the work had not been done to stop the big shifting, the deaths would have happened.

And so, yes, we have a strong sense that the Juan de Fuca locked plate problem needs to be calmed immediately, and we begin easing it immediately. We put Vortex healing energies on that area, and we play the Musical Rapture.

*See Glossary on Vortexes and Musical Rapture.

We work very hard to reduce the stress, and when we are satisfied, we are surprised to have visitors. Barbara can see them even though they are not in the third dimension. Three Pleiadian males. They have come to say they are pleased. This is our first indication that the Pleiadians have helped with the Juan de Fuca Plate and we are happy. Mother Earth needs all the help she can get!

Margaret Channeling to ask Yolanda of the Pleiades if we have done enough:

Answer: Yes, you have done enough. Let it rest. Let it be in its natural state – the blanket of calm. Ease and grace. Slowness, expansion, relaxation, calm.

Flow the energy. Sail on the winds of change, expansion, compassion. Look outwards. Follow your heart. Use your allies to make the world a better place – the dolphins, whales, the angels, the trees, the clouds, the waters, the rainbows, the shells, the crystals and stones, the ferns, the fire, the lava, the Brothers and Sisters of the Higher Worlds waiting to join forces.

Yolanda comments on Barbara seeing the three Pleiadian males and I do not:

When looking for us, you do not find us. We find you hard at work for Mother Earth. Celebrate her wonder. Acknowledge her gift to all life forms on the planet. Bow deeply in appreciation. If all humanity would stop and say thank you to the planet and stand in appreciation, all storms would stop and all wars would cease.

Let us knit together the many realities. All are one. There are no differences. The life love force moves through all as the plants grow and the sun shines. Movement and Balance, moving forward.

Peace, Love, Life. Peace, a salve for Mother Earth.

From Barbara:

When we start using the Internet to investigate earth movements in the Pacific, we find maps showing us where these earthquakes are taking place. There seems to be a consistency in that certain locations are having earthquakes over and over again. Often the Pacific coast itself would be showing earthquakes. For example, certain locations in Peru, Chile, Guatemala, Tonga, Papua New Guinea, Indonesia, Japan, Siberia, Alaska, California.

I call these locations hinge rattlings. Some are tightening, some are loosening. In any case, they are not quiet.

As mentioned in Chapter 3, we have called on the Aborigines to help us ease stress at plate hinges for Japan. Well, we want to call on the Aborigines to help us with all of the Pacific, and yes, we do call on them to help.

And then we learn of help coming from the Higher Worlds in the form of a project called Way of Peace. This project specializes in the waters of the world being given special energy.

Daily, hourly, every molecule of earth water is given this special energy and it is being filtered into humanity's hearts and minds. We are told that when every heart and mind can sufficiently grasp the concept of the Way of Peace, we can expect peace from humanity as well as from Mother Earth. We realize this will take time.

We need to tell you more about the Way of Peace project. It is aided by Light coming to Mother Earth via a unique portal in the Tetons. The Kaitiaki, New Zealand guardians of the land, water, plants and animals, are involved. During the initial infusion of the Way of Peace into water, the Kaitiaki were performing a 6,500-year-old Waitaha Water Ceremony. Incidentally, Dr. Masaru Emoto, world famous for healing the waters of the world, died at the time of the big water ceremony. We feel he left for the Higher Worlds knowing about the ceremony and he will be actively working from the Other Side for the world and humanity.

From Margaret:

In meditation, I have my crystals and the Vortexes as I settle into a deep love focus for the plates of the Pacific Ocean that need peace and stability. I feel the ocean water swelling with love. I think of the Kaitiaki people of New Zealand praying for the Way of Peace for the earth waters. Suddenly I am swept up into a powerful force field of energy that is positive, all loving. I feel Balance, Protection, Growth, Healing.

Light envelopes me and all life forms of the Pacific -- water, air, fire, land. I greet the powerful guardians of Mount Fuji, Chugash, Mount Shasta, the Tetons, Machu Picchu, Uluru, and Pele of Kilauea. I greet all the guardians of the Pacific and beyond. The feeling is off world. I am simultaneously in space and in the water. Everything is the frequency of Joy, Love and Peace. It is as if I have entered through a new portal that opened to the Kaitiaki ceremony for healing the world waters. This frequency is all balance and acceptance, a paradise on land and sea reachable by everyone who thinks on the true essence of the Pacific which is Peace. The frequency of water is love expressed in hexagonal crystalline form.

My crystals are smiling and I know they feel the connections in frequency of the ceremony and water. Love frequency. Hexagonal quartz crystals, frozen water crystals -- all expressing, all holding the frequency of Love. This frequency is available for the entire planet.

Now the Whales speak.

We are the Guides. Use this frequency of love for the planet. It is available. Should you wish to dip into this frequency, you will find the world of the past, the future, the now. Here is the healing vibration for Mother Earth and all her life forms. This frequency is the key to opening the portal. You can find the door by placing the planet first in your heart's thoughts. Pick up the trade winds. Find the currents. It is all there in your heart. It is frequency that takes you there, not a mental map.

Are others speaking I ask?

Yes, the Pleiadians, the Sirians, Whale friends in space.

We must help bring the Way of Peace energy to all living on Mother Earth. We will continue working on the Pacific plates until we are satisfied we are no longer needed.

Incidentally, at the same time we are working with the Way of Peace energy, a tremendous cyclone is approaching Australia. We ask the Aborigines to help calm it and they agree. We think that if we can ease pressure on the Pacific plates to cut down on earthquakes, we can also use sound/love music to cut down the force of winds ready to hit Australia.

The Internet has maps showing us exactly where the cyclone will hit Australia coming off the Pacific, and we are told the exact times of approach and the intensity of the winds. With the Aborigines playing didgeridoos, we use the cosmic Paneurhythmy music and our minds to send out thoughts of tempering the wind.

*See Glossary: Paneurhythmy music.

Guess what! Before reaching land, the winds diminished so that the category of the cyclone was dropped and dropped and dropped. Even some alerts were cancelled. The weather became manageable.

And so, look what can be done to help in times of urgency!

Emma Channeling to Margaret:

Yes, you have made a difference. Weather intensity can be altered by positive energy. Send love, balance frequencies to blanket the area.

The selection of Paneurhythmy music is good. There is a circular motion to the music following the dance which can fit into the rhythm patterns of the storm.

(As I am listening to the Paneurhythmy music, with my mind, I am projecting circular dancing of the Bulgarians who introduced this music to the world.)

Love Lacings can alter the texture of the storm. Gaps and holes and interlude affect it.

High frequency human action patterns of dancing and playing Paneurhythmy music follow Nature. To strive for balance, the storm will not go into excessive overload when faced with positive love frequencies.

All must be considered. All must be understood in the complexities of things.

With love to the planet,
Emma

CHAPTER 5

HAWAII, THE BIG ISLAND

Sometimes coincidences are a surprise. But, are they really coincidences, or have they have been set up by the Higher Worlds? Sometimes a 'coincidence' happens a long time before the reason becomes apparent.

From Barbara:

About thirteen years ago, when we are present at the Ringing of the Peace Bell at the United Nations in New York City, we meet for the first time Eric Salvisberg living in southern France who is on his way to the Statue of Liberty after the UN Peace Bell event is over. We say we would like to go with him and we do. Years later, 2012, Margaret is at Mount Shasta when unexpectedly she sees a familiar face, Eric Salvisberg of the Peace Bell Ringing in New York. She says, "Are you my friend?", and he replies, "Yes, Margaret, I am."

Now, January 15, 2015, another 'coincidence' is ready to fit. From southern France, Eric writes us that a Star Visitor Sanctuary was officially created one year ago, June 27, 2014, on the Big Island of Hawaii. He gives us a website with a video of the June 27 ceremony. We have never heard of a Star Visitor Sanctuary, but this sounds interesting.

Now we learn something startling. On June 27, one year ago, the same day as the official ceremony for creating a sanctuary for extraterrestrials to visit the earth, lava begins to flow downward from a vent in Kilauea Volcano toward Pahoa, a town that has road access to the sanctuary area.

Why is this happening?

We are told that the extraterrestrials, or at least some of them, will be from the Pleiades, home of ancient ancestors of the Hawaiians. And so the visitors will be meeting as friends their ancient relatives. Today, millions have cellphones and Internet access, which means the world would quickly hear about this meeting in friendship.

Well, with lava flowing, wouldn't the planned meeting be interrupted? Via the Internet, we begin watching the lava flow as well as listening to daily announcements from the Hawaii County Civil Defense. The first announcement we hear is that the lava flow has stopped moving about .6 miles from the active center of Pahoa. We want to encourage this lava halt and we put our mind on stopping the flow. For one week it ceases and then it starts again.

We have to ask ourselves why this lava started flowing on the very day the Star Visitor Sanctuary is announced. We have many questions and we are not satisfied with any answers.

With the thought that powerful Vortex energy may help stem the lava flow, we send a Vortex booklet to an acquaintance living in Pahoa.

From Margaret:

Channeling to Goddess Pele whose home is Kilauea:

Dear Pele, Barbara says we are to watch from a distance the vent erupting from Kilauea Volcano. Can you comment on the lava flow or anything we should know?

Pele: Wait. Observe.

There is a distance between you and Pahoa. The Vortexes make the bridge. It is perfect they are on their way in a tight package. The Vortex Booklet.

Everything is in order. You have thrown the Vortex Ring into the center. Perfect timing. Step back and relax. Find your own lava (mind) flow and let the Kilauea lava flow be in its perfection, its schedule, its consequence.

You gave the gift of Vortexes. When you visited me earlier in 2013, you gave me the gift of Vortexes. Energy. All is energy. Fire. All is fire. Water. All is water. Life. All is one.

Love. All is love.

From Barbara:

To establish a sanctuary in Pele's stronghold is curious. If the lava continues to encroach, will the sanctuary be relocated?

Emma Channeling to Margaret:

Pele's lava flow is Pele's agenda, not yours. Do not put static on the line. Support her endeavor of growing land, flowers, trees, ferns, animals, fish and birds within her environment which is quite a large jurisdiction, the rim of the Pacific.

Rattling the nerves upsets the plates. Calm the frequency. Keep all in order. Delete franticness. Go for smooth sailing. Do not go out in turbulent waters. Watch. Wait. Be prepared.

As always, Emma of the Higher Worlds.

I find myself continuing to worry, watching the volcano still coming close to Pahoa.

The Dolphins speak:

Put your mind away. Calm the waters of your thoughts. Yes, this is natural in its own way.

Pele speaks again:

Let it be. Let Nature take its course. If you build a house or commercial center on a side of a volcano, well, the volcano goes with the territory. One aspect of living in Paradise is that fire is always close by and present. But, abundant life is present as well.

The Pacific Dolphins add:

Hawaii is the center of the wheel of the Pacific. The center spin. The center of all goodwill, the Aloha spreading outwards. What a perfect landing place. A Galactic Welcome. No one is a stranger. All are welcome who come in Peace. That is our line. Pele is above, within and below us. She is of her own essence. The bottom line is Pele. Those who come and those who go and those who stay – she holds the lease.

With love from the Dolphins.

Emma comments:

Wait and observe. It was slowed. The land is vast. If it moves forward, perhaps it will not be as wide.

Pele is in charge. We are appreciative of off-world help. The world is watching. There is no panic from the people.

Again from the Dolphins:

Do not fret. All will be revealed in good time. Continue sending love to Hawaii, the Nature Kingdom, the plants, the trees, the lava, the sea life, birds – all abundant. Love not Fear.

Blanket of calmness and compassion for all living things. That is the resonance of Hawaii. You have old connections –- the ferns and their sacred geometry of creation, evolvement, growth. Fire to Stone to Soil to Life. Look at the drama unfolding.

From Pele:

I look at the hearts of the people and they want peace on the planet, peace on this island. This vision benefits all and I am for that. The ones who welcome others do not wish confrontations, conflicts, but openness, a welcoming, an open Spirit, the essence of Hawaii.

Those who respect me respect Mother Earth and open their hearts to welcome ancient ancestors of those who live here.

The volcanoes are all connected. The people are all connected – those that wait, those that visit, those that plant new dreams.

My love, my lava flows out to the people. I feel the resonance in the hearts of those attempting to open the meeting place.

No one fears the volcano. You were taught about the fire. It is all about love and respect. Carry a line and you can be a part of all things. It is a balanced walk. It is easier in higher dimensions. Love frequency is the path. Stay centered in that.

There are changes coming. Humans need to be with, work with, breathe with the active volcanoes, the shifting plates. The key is the calmness and respect in the hearts of those involved. Follow the heart path. See the Rainbow. Nature and human Nature become one. The orchid is the seal. The Rainbow is the bridge.

With love to those who care, from Goddess Pele of the Volcano — Being and Power.

Note from Barbara:

As we are constructing this chapter, the volcano called Mauna Loa is beginning to sputter a bit. This is a massive volcano on the Big Island of Hawaii. When we were there several years ago, we drove miles and miles and miles along the flank of Mauna Loa who was quiet. However, along the way we saw black boulders that had been flung from the volcano when it was erupting. As Pele has been saying, there is more than the explosion. There is new land, new soils for the ferns to grow, and other plants.

It is now May 2 and as we are editing this chapter, we realize more needs to be said. There is a sunken center to Kilauea Volcano and it is here where a second eruption has happened. It looks like a big circular lake of lava. Earlier at night, visitors could locate themselves at the edge of the sunken center to watch brilliant fires rising from below. The red color was spectacular in the dark of night.

But now, less than two weeks ago, this lake of lava has begun to rise. Everyone has been rushing to see it. We could watch this rising from the Internet and it has been remarkable to see the lava reaching the top and overflowing. But, what will happen next? Will it continue to rise? This means it will flow downward. What will it reach? Yes, this is a spectacular event to see. What will we see tomorrow?

Well, 'tomorrow' has come and the lava has dropped and cannot be seen. Where has it gone? We cannot answer this. Can anyone?

As an aside, we are beginning to think we should change the name of this chapter to World Volcanic Eruptions. Just now we are learning about a volcano in the Pacific about 300 miles off the coast of Oregon. For a week, this region has been showing earthquakes, a great many little ones, and this indicates the movement of magma. The ocean floor has also dropped. When we searched the Internet for the volcano off Oregon, guess what we learned?! It is located near the Juan de Fuca area. Oh dear!

CHAPTER 6

LOS ANGELES CONSCIOUS LIFE EXPO

F rom Barbara:

February 6, 2015, 4:15 a.m., a taxi picks us up to drive us to the airport for a 6 a.m. flight to begin our journey to a conference in Los Angeles called the Conscious Life Expo. Why are we going? Two reasons. To be with people whose energies are mainly positive. They would be good candidates for receiving the Vortexes introduced by Native Americans. These are powerful combined energies from other worlds supporting Mother Earth. People attending the conference are coming from all over the world and their minds tend to be positive and fresh, ready to receive what we will give them. The second reason is to join our energies with them. We are all working to help Mother Earth.

When we begin our journey, snow, which seems to be enjoying us, is still sleeping as we climb into the taxi and ride along on clear roads. Good! Margaret, who has been brought up in the South, has worries that the black roads we will use may have black ice. No. That is the custom of the South and not so much here.

When we reach the airport, even though it is early, a number of passengers are already here for an early flight to somewhere. We have our boarding passes, earlier printed off the Internet, and so we go directly to Security, which moves us along quickly enough. Soon we are at our gate waiting to board a plane resting since its flight from Canada, probably yesterday.

This is an old plane that Margaret has interpreted as having a name pronounced somewhat like Bombardier. I tell her I will be the tail gunner. When we board, I expect it may be loaded with negative energies, but no, we only join big shaking and shuttering accompanied by roars from the motor.

We are headed on this rickety plane toward New Jersey's Newark Liberty airport to catch a direct flight to Los Angeles LAX airport. We know there is little time at Newark's airport to switch to the next plane. Guess what! We are flying very slowly. In fact, we are so slow, we feel passengers at Newark are probably already boarding the Los Angeles plane.

When we arrive at the Newark airport, we must wait with others for a baggage man to retrieve our bags from the tail of the plane and bring them in a big cart to us waiting on the runway. An airport man grabs me and motions for me to climb steps with him to reach the terminal interior and a waiting passenger cart. But, what about Margaret? She doesn't yet have her bag and I don't have mine. Never mind, I am told, she will not be left behind. And so, with worry, I board the waiting passenger cart to be wheeled to an elevator that takes me upstairs to stop beside a steep stairway. Where is Margaret???? Will she be taking the stairs to reach us? The cart man tells me not to worry and he rushes downstairs as I wait and worry.

Well, there is no problem. Margaret appears with the cart man carrying our bags which he puts in the cart, along with Margaret, and we are soon on our way 'flying' down the corridors to our plane.

Yes! We reach it in time!!! Most passengers are already on board but we reach it in time. Whew!!! Without the cart man, we could have never reached the plane. As early as when we originally okayed our flights, we did not object to the short time between plane transfers.

By the way, the entire journey going and returning is free for us because of prior flight mileage.

This plane to Los Angeles we are on is comfortable, a rather new plane. It is large, with three passengers per row on each side. And, it is full. Is everyone going to the big Conscious Life Expo conference? We have been told to expect a great many.

In any case, we are on our way, and we sit back and relax while the pilot flies us above the clouds for most of the journey. I close my eyes and sleep.

Arrival at the LAX airport is easy enough. We walk through the terminal with our bags searching for the Information booth, and before we find the booth, we meet a loquacious elderly male wearing a big cowboy hat who says he works for the airport and he will escort us to the proper exit to reach the free shuttle that will take us to the Hilton Hotel where we will be staying and where the conference will be held.

People are friendly. One feels this, and one feels a relaxed manner here. As far as we are concerned, for us, California has started out on a good footing.

When we reach the proper exit to find the Hilton shuttle, we are told to walk out the door, turn left and watch for red signs. The shuttle will be blue and it will stop at the red signs. Yes! We follow these instructions and our shuttle comes quickly enough. We are soon at the front desk receiving keys to our room, which has been arranged by the conference. We will be on the fifth floor close to the elevator, and when we have put our bags in the room, we search for the dining room. We are hungry!

After eating, we begin looking for the conference that is being held in our hotel, but where? This hotel is HUGE. Where are posters announcing the location of this thirteenth annual conference? We have been told thousands will attend. Maybe the same ones attend yearly, so there is no need for signs. In any case, we ask the hotel's front desk for information and we are soon on our way downstairs and then upstairs and here and there. YES, this conference is BIG. Many, many are setting up tables of their merchandise to sell. Even though we are not allowed to enter unless we are part of this setting up, we do pass a display of many GORGEOUS CRYSTALS! WOW! I have never such a MAGNIFICENT display. Even the crystals seem happy displaying themselves.

We have in our hands powerful energy Vortexes given to us by Chief Golden Light Eagle and we begin handing them out. On the back are the words, 'Combined energies from other worlds out there who support Mother Earth'.

When 6 p.m. approaches, we have found our way to a large room ready to open the conference with a special program for Dr. Masaru Emoto who died last year on October 17. He was my friend and, because Margaret and I are in daily contact with Japan by SKYPE, when we learned about Dr. Emoto's illness, we followed his progress. First, we learned he was hospitalized in China and then he was returned to Japan where he died. As a special tribute to him, we have written about him at the beginning of our new book, 2014 World Journals. We learned only last week that this Los Angeles conference will be honoring him.

A big screen in the conference room shows us videos of frozen water molecules. Speakers come to a microphone to praise this man's wonderful contribution to humanity by demonstrating that water has a consciousness that can help humanity to bring peace and love to the planet. No one is quick to leave the opening of this conference!

February 7, Saturday:

With an eighty-one page conference brochure in our hands, we begin today by 'tasting' what the conference has to offer. There are SO MANY speakers and presenters to choose from!

Should we listen to a lecture about pocket stones and gemstone jewelry? Or about protecting your energy by frequency elevation? Or listening to the use of acupressure, Vita Water and Nano Herbs? The latter grabs our top interest because we will listen to water healing, and we are strong supporters of water with its proven consciousness.

What is Nano Vita water? We have never heard of this water. We know nothing and that is one big reason why we should listen to Dr. Luke Cua speak. We watch as this Chinese doctor enters the lecture room and we see he is self-assured as he begins speaking in clear and understandable English. We know he has had much practice speaking in front of audiences.

Of immediate interest is his explanation that traditional acupuncture can be reduced from using hundreds of needles to zero needles. Really? He says there are twelve primary acupuncture points that reveal the condition of the spleen, liver, kidney, heart, lungs, etc.

After Dr. Cua's lecture, we locate his healing space, and I take off my shoes and socks so that a small, metal, coin-shaped button can be moved from one acupuncture place to another. A thin 'phone line' is attached to the button and this 'phone line' is attached to a computer that begins immediately to register information being sent to it.

Within minutes, the body is tested. Then the computer prints out what the doctor needs to address, such as the functioning of the lungs, kidneys, etc. Even though I could not read my chart because I had never seen such a chart, I could realize that some of my body functions would seem normal and some would not.

In any case, I WAS IMPRESSED WITH DOCTOR LUKE CUA.

From him, for the improvement of my health, I have brought home Nano Vita water, herbal pills, and a special light. Three weeks afterward, as I am sitting here writing this to you, I am assessing the use of what I have brought home and I feel a health improvement.

*See Glossary for Dr. Luke Cua information.

As for the conference itself, there were many points of interest, and I was very happy to attend. Even though it has been offered for 13 years, the air is fresh and the atmosphere is creative.

From Margaret:

Today is February 5 and we leave tomorrow to attend the Los Angeles Conscious Life Expo 2015. A blizzard is predicted for tomorrow with four to eight inches of snow. At 4:00 a.m., we are to go by taxi to the airport. What are we to do? Maybe we cannot even reach the airport. The Higher Worlds tell me to pack and proceed to go.

February 6, the sun rises and we thank the sun for taking away the blizzard. It has disappeared! It never happened!

The Higher Worlds want us to go to the big conference in Los Angeles to give out Vortex energies. There will be those attending who will be taking these energies to the world. We will be mindful we are carrying these energies as we fly coast to coast.

We also know we are flying to the City of Angeles, and focus will be on the Angelic presence. There are many levels to this trip, and on arrival, we will come with positive energies of Peace, Love and Light.

We have put aside thoughts on reviewing earthquakes, volcanoes, lava flows, solar happenings, and weather conditions. Also, thoughts of nearby fault lines and tectonic plate interaction hazards have been wiped clean. All anxiety and worries have been wiped clean.

On February 6, when the plane flies over Los Angeles, I place Vortexes on the energy field of the city and surrounding area.

What is interesting to me is that when we have settled in the hotel where we will be staying and we are finding the conference rooms, we run into a young man whom we met at the Loveland, Colorado, Star Knowledge Conference last November. How amazing!

We give him the Vortexes and he thanks us. When we begin chatting, he warns us not to speak or think negatively about Mother Earth because that will bring in negative energy. We quite understand his warning and we assure him we have dismissed thinking about earthquakes, harsh weather, etc. We soon learn that those attending the conference carry the same strong positive field. Good.

It is not long before we meet Robert Quicksilver, Executive Producer of the conference. A couple months ago, we spoke on the phone with him, and today he cordially tells us he is pleased we are here. We have with us our book, 2014 World Journals, and we open it to show him our special tribute to Dr. Emoto who will be honored tonight. Later, we give him a copy of our book and Vortexes. For me, the conference is already overwhelming and it hasn't begun yet. I link to the Angels, the people of the world, the dolphins and whales, and to Mother Earth.

During the course of the conference, I attend a fascinating lecture by Ben Davidson on the sun's relationship to the earth's electrical field and its effect on weather. On the Internet, I have been following his morning news reports. Later, when waiting to attend his workshop, I stand in line with a woman and begin speaking to her. I tell her I have been following Davidson's website broadcasts and I think they are outstanding. I am a great fan. One reason why I have come to Los Angeles is to hear him speak. The lady smiles and says she is his mother and she invites me to join her and sit with the family. Afterward, I give members of the family the Vortexes as well as Ben Davidson. Also, I give him our new book, 2014 World Journals. It is the last one I have with me and it feels special to give it to him.

Later, when I am writing my notes, I think of the crowds of people here in L.A. – high healers and intuitives, artists and musicians, medicine people – all self-possessed, balanced, aware, friendly, outgoing, and very sharp.

When we attend a two-hour tribute to Dr. Masaru Emoto in the La Jolla Room, I find this formal room to be decorated with his photos and large screens showing films of water crystals and sea life. The ceremony opens with the blessing of water and a moment of love and gratitude to water and Dr. Emoto. Tom Kenyon sounds a crystal bowl and sings a message from the whales. Then, the "Song of the Ocean" is sung by a female vocalist and The Agape International Choir sings powerful jubilant songs of love, grace and power.

When we leave the celebration, each is given blessed water. We will always remember the wonderful tribute tonight to Dr. Emoto.

This morning I speak with a young technician setting up conference rooms and audio equipment. He belongs to the Agape International Spiritual Center, and I say to him how impressed we were with last night's singing of the Agape Choir.

I tell him I think there is a musical link between the East Coast Brooklyn Tabernacle Choir and the West Coast Agape Choir, both together making a rainbow arch of love across the country. He says the Agape Spiritual Center belongs both to this country and to the world. It is international and everyone comes from everywhere. Agape, meaning love, spreads around the world.

Wow, what a delight!! Yes, the love rainbow goes around the world.

I attend a crystals and gemstone lecture given by speaker Lyra who says before she begins speaking that she wants energy balance in the room. Females are at the front and she moves males forward to balance them. I feel the energy in the room change. She has given us a lesson on balance. Female energy and male energy balance.

In the early afternoon, we attend Dr. Luke Cua's lecture on Acupressure, Nano Herbs and Vita Water. He is bridging Western medicine and traditional Chinese medicine by using a computer system for diagnosing the body. We find him very informative, a person who is a scientist and a traditional doctor. When his lecture is over, we follow him to his booth where Barbara decides to be tested and I later.

At 4:00 p.m. I attend Ben Davidson's General Workshop on Star Water: Life Outside the Earth. He gives an amazing lecture about the presence of water throughout the solar system and beyond. For me, it a delight to learn water is everywhere in the universe.

* Glossary: See Ben Davidson about Star Water.

Message from the Vortex Givers of other worlds:

We are here with you in person and in the other dimensions. The two men who caught your eye yesterday were yoga sages or star brothers. Time slowed and a connection was made. They placed their hands on their hearts when they passed you and they gave out deep love.

The electrical man for Friday from the Agape Spiritual Center gave you a worldwide view for healing. Los Angeles is all about world people. So many people from so many places, merging, melding in creativity and love, offering a perspective and adding to the whole complex. Healing, life focus, expansion, freedom, free will – everyone is enacting the drama, the enactment of the Star Laws.

From Barbara:

One last comment for this chapter. The basic concept of the Vortexes is Love which has infinite meaning, and yet the energy is all positive. Los Angeles is like a big soup to be eaten by all, and this soup is good with love and creativity. Now we have put into this soup the Vortexes, the positive energies of other worlds. This makes the soup more complex, and yet it is still positive soup to be drunk by all here.

Peace, Love and Light.

CHAPTER 7

EQUINOX, SOLAR ECLIPSE, UN PEACE BELL ~ NEW YORK CITY

F rom Barbara:

March 19, Thursday, Joan Lenhard of A1 Elite Taxi picks us up a couple minutes before 7:30 a.m. to drive us to the train station to ride the Amtrak to New York City for an intensive Friday of appointments and activity. When that is finished, the train will return us to our book writing, etc., etc.

Joan is cheerful and friendly and we love taking a taxi with her. Earlier, she told us she would not be available but she has confirmed another driver for us. However, guess who is here? Joan. Hurray! A good way to start our journey.

We climb into her van and she is apologizing that the inside of her cab is dirty. To us, it looks just fine. We are happy she is here, and we are happy the weather is good, not snowing.

The accumulated 95 inches of snow are good enough for an entire winter, and we are willing to see no more! February, we are told, has been the coldest February month on record.

In fact, we have taken the train rather than a plane because we MUST be in NYC tomorrow. Trains can usually 'get through' all kinds of weather, but, planes? There have been a lot of weather cancellations this winter!

And so, we are taking the train this morning, and when we arrive at the station early for our 8:36 a.m. departure, we sit and wait patiently and watch those who will be riding with us. At first, few are here, but newcomers begin dribbling in until about forty are here by the time our train arrives.

The train station manager announces our train will be only a few minutes late, and we are happy about that. We sit and watch passing freight trains with priority over passenger trains. How many freight cars are attached to the train just now passing the station? Maybe 200. We look at the huge, black containers and we wonder what is in them. Where are they going?

When the station manager announces our train is ready to arrive, we passengers file outside to wait. Strong wind and freezing temperatures catch us. We are beginning to be spoiled by a week of acceptable temperatures and a more or less cessation of a lot of snow falling. In fact, the main topic centering on weather is that spring should be on the way! Wouldn't it be wonderful to stop wearing winter clothes!

Yes, here comes the train and we New York City bound passengers are told to board near the front of the train. A train door opens and a uniformed coachman wearing a black hat climbs down the train steps to look at our tickets and usher us aboard. When we enter, Margaret and I look for seats on the right side of the train in order to see water headed toward the Hudson River. After Albany we will turn south and go 2 1/2 hours along the Hudson to NYC.

We are in for a surprise. When we reach the first water, long before the Hudson, we see the water is covered with ice! The land is covered with snow. It is time for spring migration of ducks and geese, etc. They cannot stop here! They cannot swim in the water for protection from land animals and there is nothing for them to eat! What can they do? Turn back? Turn toward the south? As we look out the train windows, Margaret and I are somber.

When we reach Albany and then cross the bridge to begin following the Hudson River, we see that the ice has buckled so that the formation is rough, thick. I have never seen such river ice. Even warmer temperatures would not produce an easy melting process.

We see no boats on the Hudson. We think about this and overseas cargo coming from Europe. When this cargo reaches New York City and needs to start traveling north on the Hudson, what happens to the cargo if boats cannot travel on the Hudson? We see no operating icebreakers, but when we return on Saturday, we see about five. They will have a big job to do!

When our train reaches Penn Station in New York City, it is the end of the ride for everyone, and we disembark with our baggage to go upstairs to the main lobby where we head toward a small delicatessen to buy egg salad sandwiches and cranberry juice. This place has three small, round tables and high chairs. One of the three tables is free. Good! We spread out our food to eat. We are hungry.

When the food has been devoured, we head toward a nearby Information booth to ask how to easily reach the Pennsylvania Hotel where we will be staying two nights. We know it is very close to the train station. A NYC map shows us it's about two blocks away. Well, when we follow the Information booth's directions, we realize the hotel is across the street from the station! Wow! Within minutes, we are at the Front Desk. We are given keys to our prepaid room on the 11th floor.

And yes, we are happy we have arranged the room beforehand. There are 'zillions' of people milling around the ground floor. Are they are all staying here? This is a big hotel, but it is THAT big?

We have an appointment to meet Dr. Luke Cua at a New Life Expo exhibition happening this weekend on the eighteen floor of this hotel.

Is everyone staying here? We see groups of youth and we learn there are sports competitions happening near the hotel. Well, we have a hotel room and we are happy about that.

March 20, Friday, the Equinox:

This morning we will meet Marianne Trost, my niece whom I have not seen for a long time. She is a coach for women lawyers and she moves around the country as an adviser. To meet her, Margaret and I cross the street to Penn Station and find our way to the New Jersey train ticket area where we seat ourselves in the waiting area. We have a good view of everyone entering the waiting area and so we feel certain we will see Marianne.

Beside us is a man who looks as if he has made the waiting area his home. He welcomes us and we welcome him and soon we are talking back and forth with him. Fun!

Many are entering the waiting area, sitting, then lining up for trains when departures are announced. It is 10:30 a.m. this Friday morning, and many are going somewhere, probably for the weekend. Does this mean they do not work on Friday?

At 11 a.m. Marianne comes racing toward us, apologizing for being late. 'People-viewing' has been fun. Not often do we sit in a train station looking at people.

Marianne tells us she has just been invited to go to Puerto Rico to speak with women lawyers who want advice. One Puerto Rican lawyer was selected to come to New York City to judge the who, what, etc. of Marianne and this woman has found Marianne to be acceptable. So, Marianne has been invited and she is excited to go to Puerto Rico. It is a new challenge.

When her train is announced, she takes via her cell phone a photo of we three sitting together. Fun! An instantaneous snap shot! Society has graduated from the days when one had to race to the photo shop to have a photo developed. Instantaneous is the action now.

At 3 p.m., when we go upstairs to see Dr. Luke Cua, we meet his wife Irene who remembers us from February when we were at the Expo in Los Angeles. She excitedly hugs us and it is fun meeting her again. We have talked several times on the phone.

As mentioned earlier, Dr. Cua practices traditional Chinese medicine and concentrates on healing with the use of special water, light, and natural Chinese roots and herbs. Margaret and I have followed his advice given to us in Los Angeles, and we feel a health improvement within us.

And so, yes, we have an enjoyable few minutes with Dr. Cua and his wife at their booth. While we are there, several health seekers have paused to look at literature, and I comment to them that Dr. Cua is 'the best'!

---

5 p.m., we take a taxi from the Pennsylvania Hotel to the United Nations, and this is fun. The driver is from Nigeria, and although we have not visited his African country, we tell him we will be mentioning at the UN the children of Uganda whom we have visited last year. He is pleased and he says the children will never forget that we visited them.

Today is the March Equinox, and that is the reason why today we are going to the United Nations. Since 1997, I have been invited every year to attend the ringing of the Peace Bell at the March Equinox, and so, here I am again, at the UN. This year, the Equinox is at 6:45 p.m. in NYC, a moment when the sun shines directly on the Equator, which makes night and day almost equal.

Deceased John McConnell, founder of Earth Day at the Equinox, invited me to attend in 1997, and when he was too old to go to the

UN for the ringing of the Peace Bell, Margaret and I would buy a big birthday card for all to sign at the bell ringing. Then we would mail it to Denver, Colorado, where he and his wife lived. Incidentally, his birthday was March 22, and so he was an 'Equinox' man.

When the Nigerian taxi driver leaves us at the UN, we join others who will be at the bell-ringing ceremony, and I learn that the traditional peace bell will not be rung this year. The intention was to move it from the Rose Garden to its original location, but the movers ran into difficulties. The bell could not be in place for the time of the ceremony. And so, to solve the bell-ringing problem, each of us is given a tiny peace bell to ring at the moment of the Equinox.

Well, when a solution to a problem is found, there is need to accept it and not fuss. Only smiles. Today is a very special day. More special than just the Equinox. Today is a total solar eclipse and a new moon day. When the three energies are put together, esoterically, spiritually, a door is opened, and a new pattern is here on the earth. This can be a good pattern, depending on how mankind reacts.

I feel the new pattern is a good pattern because I notice that most of those I am encountering are smiling rather than frowning. Good! We need smiles! Mother Earth has been hammered by negativity.

At the bell ringing ceremony every year children play violins, and they are here for this Equinox. Most are girls whose ages are between 4 and 12, and they are wearing white, silk dresses. When the music is too lively, the youngest who cannot keep up poise their bows on the violin strings. Their leader, who is a short Asian woman, has fantastic energy as she plays her violin and at the same time conducts the children.

Just before the 6:45 p.m. Equinox, I am invited to speak and I stand at the mike to tell them about the Ugandan children who have paper bells at their hearts so they can be with us here at the ringing of the peace bell. They will be in bed because the Equinox in Uganda is at night when it is 6:45 p.m. in New York City. While I am speaking, Margaret holds up photos of the Ugandan children for all to see.

Now I explain to those assembled that the United Nations has designated this year of 2015 to be the International Year of Light and Light Technologies. As I am speaking, Margaret shows a photograph of a man holding pills of zinc, magnesium, etc., which, when properly held, will produce energy for electricity. A voltmeter is beside the man's hand, and this meter displays energy being made. It is exciting that some day there should be no need to have light posts, etc. to bring light into our homes!

Incidentally, nearly eight weeks later there is an accident at the Indian Point Nuclear plant less than thirty miles from New York City. Fortunately, it was a minor accident compared with Chernobyl and other plant breakdowns. Nevertheless, it is worrisome. Because of our research for speaking at the UN, we have information we feel would be helpful finding a substitute for nuclear power. Apparently, only 5% of New York State power comes from Indian Point. Certainly a way can be found to supply the 5% needed when the power plant is closed down.

We know Governor Cuomo is not impressed with the Indian Point Nuclear plant. We decide to send him topics we researched for our United Nations talk.

1. Bloom Boxes create electricity.
2. In Finland, photovoltaic cells are used to create electricity.
3. An aluminum-oxygen air system produces electricity.
4. A substitute for producing electricity is by combining paper with small amounts of zinc, potassium, calcium and magnesium, copper and aluminum.

All in all, I think our trip to New York City has been successful!

From Margaret:

March 19, 7:05 p.m.:

Tonight when we are in our New York City Pennsylvania Hotel room, a friend phones to say there are orca whales spotted off the Oregon coast -- three babies, one mother and one grandmother. A couple years ago, 2013, when we were at the United Nations for the Ringing of the Peace Bell, a woman announced that a dolphin had been seen in the nearby East River. This was so unusual, even the newspapers announced it.

Is there a connection here between the Equinox and the Whales and Dolphins?

I ask them to comment:

Whale Channeling: *Welcome to New York City, the land of ice and snow. We see you are on the East Coast with the gathering of the world here. East Coast, West Coast, Hawaii, Japan, Oregon – Whale Nation Movement and Balance.*

The Earth creatures are moving and sending out their messages. Tomorrow is the New Moon of the Eagle. We saw you were watching for Eagles on your train ride following the Mohawk River to the Hudson River down to New York City.

Blessings for the day of Balance when all the world is balanced and looking forward to Peace and Harmony. Little ones (whale babies) coming on (being born), showing Mother Earth's progression of Life. All want to swim, to be in her frequencies from the cold of Alaska to the warmth of Hawaii and everywhere in-between.

Bless the new whales, the new children, the new life coming into the Northern Hemisphere. There is the feeling of spring even in the snow and ice going south down the Hudson.

Love to you. Movement and Balance, Strength, Health and Happiness.

With love, The Whales

PS from Margaret: Before leaving for NYC, I see three robins welcoming spring in the North.

March 20, 5:30 a.m.

The New Moon Solar Eclipse begins at 3:41 a.m. New York time and ends at 7.50 a.m. Right now it is 5:30 a.m. and I am in the middle of it. This grand event is only visible in northern Europe and the Arctic and I am here in New York City so I am out of view of it but I can feel it.

I think on an eclipse message of Father Sun given to the Native Americans saying all things change in a blink of an eye. Each eclipse is important because of strong energies coming in, and so one needs to prepare because there will be Mother Earth changes. Later, while searching the Internet, I find a spectacular video capturing how it feels to witness such an event.

*Glossary: Eclipse video.

I find the feeling of New York City is energetic yet calm, balanced, enthusiastic. Even before reaching New York City, I enjoy seeing ice diamonds sparkling in the sunlight on the frozen Hudson River. When it is open water, I see sunlight white and dancing on the Hudson. With my mind, I spin the Vortexes, thinking of the river, blessing the river, blessing the day, blessing the high intensity sunlight.

6:00 a.m., I receive a message from Father Sun referring to the Solar Eclipse.

Good morning, my dear earth friends. My Light is always constant and growing in complexity.

The Moon of the Earth delicately rotates to balance the energy of the water life forms on planet Earth. Expansion and contraction, expansion and contraction, pumping energy into the systems. The crossing of my path darkens my Light and makes it come back more intensely. (Father Sun is referring to the Solar Eclipse.)

A moment, a breath, an awareness of the wondrous system my and your Solar System takes – activity, growth, expansion of wisdom and generosity.

Shine your light as I shine mine. Beacons of Light, multi-faceted, contained within the movement and change of the planet's rotations and movement, progression within the entire universe system.

Layers and Layers of Light and Energy. Expansion and Contraction to Expansion. Vastness. Minuteness. All with the same blink of consciousness.

The Earth moon crosses my light. The awareness, celebration of the Solar Eclipse, awakens the earth people to the wonders of these times. Lenses. Take your mind and expand outward to all the planetary systems, universal systems, and then refocus the mind's lens to the magnificence of the cellular structure, the intricate world of the plants, the soil, the water, the air.

How perfectly they interact with each other with the coming of spring in the Northern Hemisphere and the going to sleep in the Southern Hemisphere. Expansion, Contraction. Expansion, Contraction. Movement and Balance. As above, so below. Light, Sound and Vibration, Life, Change, Intuition, Right Relationships, Protection, Love, Symmetry and Balance. All in wondrous perfection.

All of this revealed in a blink of an eye when the moon crosses my path at the Solar Eclipse. Light out, Light on. A deep appreciation of this wondrous event. To stop, to pause, to take in the true complexity of Light, Life, Love of My Being.

Blessings to the inhabitants of Earth today. A Solar Eclipse, an Equinox, more and more Light. Light is Love and Love is Light.

With the understanding of that, all things change and become better.
Progression in wisdom for my Solar System inhabitants.

Bless your Mother Earth for she provides you Life. We work together
and all things thrive in a Natural Way, with balanced systems. As
above, so below.

Welcome to my world, my universe, my understanding.

The Sun

I am nearly overwhelmed by the Sun's message! Such keen observation! Such power! Such love! I hope your reaction is as strong as mine!

8:00 a.m., we go downstairs for breakfast of various sweet rolls, fruit and orange juice. There are many assembled here -- Brazilian team coaches, Japanese tour groups, Russian women hostesses, etc.

We sit at tables reminiscent of the old days of jazz. On the walls are jazz musical instruments and I can still feel the music within them. Also, on the walls are two large abstract pictures, one of a jazz band and another of a formal piano concert in an opera house. I hear no music this morning but music is floating around. Memories of music are floating around.

Yes, there is a big connection between the big band era and the Pennsylvania Hotel. Famous bands earlier played here in the hotel's Café Rouge – the Dorsey Brothers, Woody Herman, Count Basie, Duke Ellington, and Glenn Miller and his band. The well-know song *Pennsylvania 6-5000* was the hotel's telephone number. How amazing! I am living today in memory.

10:30 a.m., we cross the street to Penn Station to meet Marianne Trost, a lecturer and coach for women lawyers. We have a delightful time speaking about her projects and ours. I give her Vortexes on this special day of the Equinox and Solar Eclipse.

At 2:30 p.m., we are at New Life Expo to meet Dr. Luke Cua and his wife Irene who is enthusiastic and supportive of her husband. He is an excellent diagnostician, natural healer and teacher. Yes, they are a wonderful team. How amazing to see them again in New York City following our time with them in Los Angeles.

5:00 p.m., we take a taxi to the United Nations and it is driven by a Nigerian who loves our stories about Ugandan school children. As we drive along, we watch snow falling on this first day of spring. It decorates the trees but does not build up on the streets.

At the UN, we meet Mary Carlin of the Earth Society who has arranged the event for the Ringing of the Peace Bell. She assigns a staff member to guide us through Security and then walk with us across a slippery plaza. Our destination is downstairs in the North Building, and on arrival we find many gathered.

When the ceremony begins, small children play their violins and then speakers use a mike to talk about the history of Earth Day. A young female student from India speaks about her vision of generations working together for the environment. A tall American male swimmer speaks about how he will swim two nearby toxic rivers to help bring attention to protecting the rivers and cleaning them up. I admire his heroic thoughts.

Barbara speaks about the children celebrating the ringing of the Peace Bell in Uganda by holding paper bells to their hearts while we are at the United Nations. She also explains about the UN choosing 2015 to be designated the International Year of the Light and Light-based Technologies.

At the moment of the Equinox, we ring little bells and our hearts are full of love. We think of all the bells for peace being rung around the world.

Now we listen to the small children playing their violins and then we exit the building to walk up slippery stairs across the plaza to the street to a parked taxi. The driver is Moroccan, and while we are riding along, Barbara tells him she used to live in Morocco. He is pleased and the two enjoy taking about Morocco as he takes us to the Pennsylvania Hotel.

8:30 p.m., I return briefly to the New Life Expo on the 18th floor to receive herbs from Dr. Cua's wife Irene. Again, she is so excited to see us, and she says they will return to NYC in October for an Expo. She hopes to see us again.

Our mission is accomplished. We have helped ring the Peace Bell; we have spoken to Marianne Trost; and we have met healer Dr. Cua and his wife. We have given our love and light to all the people during this important moment of the Solstice and Eclipse and we have spread out the frequency of peace.

May Peace Prevail On Earth.

CHAPTER 8
WASHINGTON, D.C.
CHERRY BLOSSOM FESTIVAL

From Margaret:

April 9:

Tomorrow, Friday, we have intended to drive to Washington, D.C. to see the Cherry Blossom Festival, but this morning the Higher Worlds suggest we begin driving today.

What an amazing idea! The weather is cold and a storm with high winds is expected late this afternoon. We can leave before the storm, make our way south toward Virginia, and stop for the night when we are tired.

Why are we traveling to Washington, D.C. at the time of the Cherry Blossom Festival? To honor the 1912 gift of the cherry trees from the Japanese people to our nation's capital and the American people.

I grew up in Washington, D.C. and the high point of every year of my youth was when the cherry blossoms came out. After I learned to drive, I drove to the Tidal Basin to walk among the beautiful, delicate trees.

There were cherry trees everywhere in Washington and when at full bloom and the winds came, the blossoms would 'rain' down. This was a joy to behold. Then we would wait for the next year for the cherry blossoms to come again.

In 2001, we were in Washington, D.C. when Japanese came to the festival and marched in the Cherry Blossom Parade. This link was made by us the previous year when we travelled to Japan in December to commemorate the beginning and the end of World War II and to place the peace frequency on the new century.

On December 7, 2000, Barbara and I went to the Yasukuni Shrine in Tokyo and then to the war history museum where we meditated and saw on the wall above us a beautiful picture of a Japanese pagoda surrounded by cherry trees in full bloom. This returned memories of my youth, and I told Barbara the love of the cherry trees is the heart link between the United States and Japan.

We told our Japanese friends they should come to Washington, D.C. in the spring of 2001 and they did! Wearing bright peace jackets, they marched in the Cherry Blossom Parade and carried banners saying May Peace Prevail On Earth as well as all the flags of the world.

Now it is the year 2015 and we are going to the Cherry Blossom Festival in Washington, D.C. to acknowledge the gift of the Japanese and the message of May Peace Prevail On Earth.

We begin driving at 2:35 p.m. and the car is packed with winter coats, raincoats and spring coats to handle any type of weather. Just now it is cold. There is an icy feel to the air. We drive down Route 15 through the magnificent mountains in southern New York and we continue into Pennsylvania. We are seeing mountains formed by layers and layers of rock reminding me of the Niagara Escarpment that was a former seabed floor lifted up with only a thin layer of soil on top and mighty layers of rock beneath. The rock is encrusted with ancient sea life, and we know we are looking at strong, positive energies.

New road construction exposes vast layers beneath her surface and we are in awe of her complexity and immense power and strength. We realize that if people could grasp the full intensity of Mother Earth and her past, present and future, they would walk respectfully on her surface.

The stones give me a message. *Come sit with a rock or rock layer and understand time and one's place in time.*

Now, here in the high mountains, we begin to experience fog. Clouds descend and soon intense fog envelops the car. Big trucks carrying heavy loads slow down and turn on their flashers. We slow down, turn on our flashers, and carefully follow white-painted lines on the road helping to guide drivers. Luckily, not many people are driving. We are relieved when the fog begins to lift and finally the sky is clear again.

When we reach Williamsport, we decide to start looking for a hotel. A bit further, we stop for the night at an excellent hotel, the Hampton Inn in Lewisburg. When I fall asleep, I honor the great mountains we have just passed. I continue feeling their strength. And I am also thinking of the rivers. We are now in the jurisdiction of the Susquehanna River which is flooded. Tomorrow we will be traveling between two powerful rivers, the Susquehanna and the Potomac. I was born near the Potomac and I love them both.

April 10:

We have a delightful breakfast watching birds at a feeder on the other side of a hotel window in front of us, and then we are on our way again. It is cold with a slight rain. We note the Susquehanna River is far over its banks and islands are under water. Trees are standing alone in the current. It is the highest level I have ever seen!

In Harrisburg, we somehow manage to navigate the confusion of roads and then we head toward Gettysburg less than fifty miles away.

As we are driving through rolling hills and fields, we use the CD player to listen to Japanese Michiko Moroi who is singing Let There Be Peace On Earth in English and Japanese. Her voice is beautiful, full of Joy, full of Love, and we were happy to meet her when she came to Washington, D.C. in 2001.

*See Glossary for Michiko Moroi music.

We are playing the music when we pass Gettysburg with its Civil War history, and we are playing it when we drive near Frederick, Maryland, which has converted its pastures and fields to commercial and government buildings and residences. When we reach Leesburg, Virginia, we see some old houses tucked away behind fences or within clusters of trees, but mostly we see new roads and residences.

Now Route 7 is coming into view, and we are close to Dulles Airport which is close to our destination, the Washington Dulles Airport Marriott Hotel. But, we discover, we are lost! We even take the same toll road twice before we find the hotel.

Our room is on the third floor and what a room! When we open the door, we see beyond our window a full chorus of cherry blossom trees in the hotel's courtyard. WOW!! The cherry blossoms are out!! Full Bloom!! At their peak!! We have reached the land of the cherry blossoms in full bloom!! Oh glory, what a sight to behold!!

We have lunch in our room viewing the cherry blossoms, and then we use an ingenious travel system of shuttle, bus, Metro to reach the Smithsonian Museum Metro stop which is close to the Tidal Basin and the cherry trees.

Now we need a taxi and when we wave to one, the driver makes a smart C-turn and swoops down and picks us up. He says he will take us to the Tidal Basin and drop us off, but we say no. We want him to drive us around the Basin to see the cherry trees. He says there is too much traffic to do this, but we say we have come all this way to see the cherry trees and he must do this. Miraculously, the traffic begins to thin and when we reach the Tidal Basin, there is no traffic.

He drives us slowly and we see the full beauty and the full range of the cherry trees. The sun comes out and lights the way.

Our driver, who is a Sikh from India living in Virginia, tells us he has three children going to college. When he returns us to the Smithsonian Metro stop, we thank him for our excellent tour which felt spontaneous, as if we were teleported 'without a feather out of place', as the birds would say.

We use the same complex travel system of Metro, bus, shuttle to return to the hotel, and along the way we talk with many friendly riders.

April 11, Saturday:

I am up early welcoming the sunrise on the official day dedicated to The Cherry Blossom Festival. I feel the sun sending the power of love to Washington, D.C. and everywhere. It is shining brilliantly. This is perfect for everyone coming to the festival.

At the Metro stop, we join happy families going to the festival, and they are light-hearted and we are light-hearted. With the help of the brilliant sun, Peace, Love and Light is everywhere.

There are hundreds, thousands going to the festival. We travel with these wonderful people until we reach the stop called Metro Center, and then we leave them and to go to our next destination, Mary's church. I feel Her strong presence.

From Barbara:

I agree 100% with Margaret's writing of our journey. My words would be the same as hers. I will write a few words about our journey to the home of Mary, mother of the Christ, and representative of the

Divine Feminine. Her home is called the Basilica Of The National Shrine Of The Immaculate Conception. A few years earlier, we visited this large basilica and we noted its warm and loving energies. The countries around the world have sponsored specific chapels for Mary. One chapel is African and the figure of Mary is black. Other chapels represent Poland, China, Ireland, etc.

To reach this holy place, we take public transportation and very quickly we are with a 'million' people who have come from all over the world to attend the Cherry Blossom Festival. The Metro is so crowded, normal schedules are thrown out the window and there are delays. However, everyone is happy and patient and peaceful. We love being with them. When it is time to travel toward the Basilica rather than to the Tidal Basin, we say goodbye to friends we have just made and they say goodbye to us in a warm manner. Now, transportation is normal, and in fact, somewhat light because everyone is going to see the cherry blossoms at the Tidal Basin.

Interesting, when we reach the Basilica, what do we see? Cherry blossoms!

Yes, our journey from beginning to end has been wonderful. Positive energy throughout. When we return to New York State, we take all this energy and send it out to all the world. That is what we want for everyone all day and all night. Only the positive.

From Margaret:

We want to send photographs of the cherry blossom trees to our friends in Japan, and so I search the Internet after our journey. What I find is amazing! The National Park Service has announced that the peak moment of the cherry tree bloom time was Friday, April 10 at 7:24 p.m. We were there less than two hours earlier. Our timing could not have been better. Mother Nature must have been guiding us. Also, we think she is the one who opened the skies to the sunshine. We learned it had been persistently overcast in Washington, D.C., but then the skies cleared and the weekend was sunny and bright.

CHAPTER 9

DOLPHINS AND WHALES
~ EARTHQUAKES

F rom Barbara:

We have been so busy with the Cherry Blossom Festival, we have
not been up-to-date on other world matters. Then we learned from
Annelies of Switzerland that 150 dolphins beached on the shores
of Japan. All but three died. We SKYPE our friend in Tokyo asking
for information and we learn that scientists who examined the dead
dolphins learned that the source of premature death was from a
disease stemming from too much intake of radiation. We are not
scientists, so our explanation may be a bit askew here. We understand
that the lungs of the dead dolphins showed no blood, and so oxygen
could not be absorbed. The dolphins died of suffocation.

It is our understanding that beneath the ruptured Fukushima nuclear
power station radiation continues to meet the waters of the Pacific.
Sea life cannot live in these polluted waters.

How can we help?

We feel we need to construct a positive thought form. We drive to
Lake Ontario listening to the positive energy of music composed by

Japanese Hiroyoshi Kawagishi. We have with us Nano Vita Water, which according to Chinese Dr. Luke Cua, has the ability to force the negative from the body. We are thinking of the dolphins that have ingested the negative energy of radiation and this has eventually killed them. They were living in water that has a consciousness. Our thought is to put Nano Vita Water into Lake Ontario, and at the same time, we will be 100% supporting thoughts that all equals one. Putting this water into the lake here is the same as putting Nano Vita Water into all the water of the world.

We two have just returned from a place of perfection, the Cherry Blossom Festival. Around us were the human energies of peace and kindness. Millions were there, joined with similar thoughts. When we put the Nano Vita Water into Lake Ontario for all the waters of the world, we consciously are carrying the powerful thoughts of peace and kindness.

It is not for us to judge what we have just done. We have done our best.

From Margaret:

I am overwhelmed with shock about the 150 dead dolphins. Can this be a warning for 2015?

I ask the dolphins to comment and they respond:

Margaret, Your emotional body is stirring up sand in the communication. Many factors affect the lives of the dolphins – the currents, the electromagnetism of earth, the guidance system, the group thought of the dolphins.

Perhaps the dolphin incident could be a mass statement to wake up the Japanese as to the precious life of the dolphins and whales. They live in a country that still kills whales.

It could be a warning to make all systems as precious as human systems. Sea life is as important as life on land. Japan is surrounded by seas.

There are underwater volcanoes that affect the water temperature and conditions. Perhaps take all of this into consideration.

How far away from the ocean is Fukushima pouring in radiation? So many factors. One or a combination. What about the storms offshore? What about the solar events? Underwater earthquakes in the nearby area? There is so much the dolphins and whales have to contend with at this time. Their beaching brings human attention to their plight in the world today.

Send love and appreciation to them. They hold greater knowledge than humans for the preservation of life on Earth. Their greatest gift is JOY and Living Life Exuberantly. They live full out. They do not hold back. They send out love with all soundings.

Your Brothers and Sisters of the Deep.

I turn to channeling Emma.

We are heavy-hearted to learn of the plight of the dolphins and whales and all the sea creatures of the Pacific. Radiation is washing everywhere. Humans have unleashed destruction that cannot be contained or stopped. Sea life is first affected. What can we do to modify the disaster?

I say to Emma, we now know the full extent of the problem.

Emma responds: You know now the full implication of human folly and recklessness. What is important is for the information to get out and for the scientific communities to work on ways to ameliorate the problem. Perhaps new technology could be developed to buffer or modify the radiation – such as extended pyramids or sacred Agnihotra fires. Perhaps contact with the Higher Worlds can bring the solution. Transformation. Reconfiguration. Absorption. Disposal.

Keep going. Pull together.

With love,
Emma

Now I want to question Master Goi about earthquakes.

Dear Master Goi, the Pacific has so many continuous earthquakes at 5.0 plus. Some are 6. and 7. Japan has earthquakes every day. Volcanoes are spewing fire and smoke, rocks and debris. Mother Earth is in turmoil. In your opinion, what is the condition of Mother Earth? Are matters getting worse? More earthquakes, more violent storms? We are very concerned. Can you give us insight?

Master Goi responds: We are going through unstable times. That is why I want the people to focus on May Peace Prevail On Earth. To come into agreement instead of ripping the world apart with feuds and violence. Each violent action causes shock waves to Mother Earth and this reverberates into earthquakes, torrential storms, mudslides. Volcanoes relieve the pressure.

Plates have to move as one part expands and the other part has to adjust. The key is the calmness of the environment, the calmness of the human environment. Tomorrow is Earth Day, and each person should send gratitude and love to Mother Earth.

Infinite Love. Infinite Gratitude. Infinite Peace within and without. May Peace Prevail On Earth for this generation and the next and the next and the next,

With Infinite Love for the people, Master Goi.

I am still anxious and I speak again with Emma.

Dear Emma, yesterday we were told by the Higher Worlds to leave the house quickly and take supplies and go to an open space to park. Can you comment?

Emma responds: It is good to have an earthquake plan practice. The earth is unsettled and earthquakes can happen anywhere.

As you prepare, others will also. Preparation and not panic. Earthquakes are not just far off, in distant places, but they are also here because of the disruption of the underlayment of the base rock foundation. This heightens the body's sensitivity to the environment.

Shorten your time span. Think day by day. Hour by hour. Spread Light as you walk. Spread Love where you walk. Do not contract in fear but expand outwards in a large field of positive energy. The sun rises, the sun sets – the blessing energy of the sun – the balance of the moon. Move through the day with the understanding of the sun and the moon. Be in harmony with the earth.

Perhaps tell others what you have just experienced in leaving the house quickly with supplies.

My love from your friend, Emma -- Right here, above, beside, within -- Love.

A message comes from Emma and the Christ:

May Peace Prevail On Earth.
Peace be with you.
Open your heart and breathe. Breathe.
Slow down anxiousness.

Walk with ease and grace. Hold that as your frequency. Calm. Movement and Balance. Strength, Health and Happiness. Crystals are here sending love. The Higher Worlds are here sending love.

Friends around the world are sending love. The flowers, the horses, the dolphins send love. Send love outwards and love comes flowing in.

Breathe with Pele. Breathe with Mother Earth. Bless, send Love to the people with health issues. Lay down the Light. Lay down the Love. Be at Peace. Be at Peace. Peace.

CHAPTER 10

WESAK FESTIVAL ~ AGNIHOTRA HEALING

F rom Barbara:

Good morning, folks, today is May 3, 2015. It is the moment of the Taurus full moon when there is strong concentration by many people to spread goodwill among mankind. A festival today is called the Wesak Festival. The custom of celebrating at this time of the full moon of May stems from the East where regard for the Buddha is strong, said to be born at this time.

Now I want to give you the Foreward of this book. "We firmly believe in what we believe and we realize you may not agree with everything we believe. Probably we would not agree with everything you agree with. But let us put aside our differences and let us be friends. It's the world that matters. Mother Earth needs help and we are trying to give it to her. That is all that is expected."

There is a place in the Himalayas called the Wesak Valley, and here, yearly, at the time of the full moon of May, a great number gather. This full moon is regarded as a time for healing, and so healing is on the thoughts of those gathered there. For me, I cannot be today at the Wesak Valley in the Himalayas, and yet, my thoughts are with those thinking healing. Will you be with me? You also do not have to be physically there in order for your thoughts, your energy, to be there.

Those who regard the Buddha say that every year Buddha brings new Light, new energy to the world. That is goodwill. You are a part of the world and I am a part of the world. Therefore, this energy, this goodwill, is ready for us to assimilate. We know that Mother Earth needs help and we can give this goodwill to her. Each in his own way. There is no set way to help. We merely have to do it.

It is believed that the Christ plays a strong part in the gathering of people in the Wesak Valley at the time of the full moon festival. If you believe in the Buddha and the Christ, so be it. If you believe in only the Buddha or only the Christ, that is okay. Let us put aside our differences and be friends working together with our energies to help Mother Earth. Goodwill is all that matters here.

I think it is a good time to tell you about Agnihotra, an ancient healing fire technique that purifies the atmosphere and also heals people. It is known in India and other places of the world.

December 2, 1984, a pesticide factory in Bhopal, India, began releasing deadly toxic gases. A half million people were exposed and thousands died. Medical facilities were minimal at best, and those exposed to the deadly gas had little chance of finding help. However, one help was available. Agnihotra.

This ancient healing fire technique that purifies the atmosphere was set up and for weeks Agnihotra fires burned. Survivors were those who sought protection with the fires. As medicine, Agnihotra ash was distributed and Agnihotra eye-drops were given out. Newspapers in India began writing about the positive effects of Agnihotra.

Do you realize that a main ingredient for healing can be the use of sound? Agnihotra fires may seem silent but they are not. They give out sound. An oscilloscope will show this.

A copper pyramid is used for burning the fire and this fire is built at sunrise and sunset, the exact two moments that have the highest healing effects of resonance, sound. Sacred chanting accompanies the sacred fires burned in a copper, pyramid-shaped pot and fed dung and rice.

*Glossary: Agnihotra.

As for the Bhopal tragedy, I want to say again that those who sat at the fire greatly benefited. Today, in many parts of the world, people regularly perform the Agnihotra fire ceremony to create a peaceful, healing atmosphere. It is said that the fire can help minimize the adverse impact of nuclear radiation.

One time I was staying in a room with two ill Australian girls at a Sai Baba Ashram in India. Agnihotra fire expert George Eggleston was also at the Ashram, and he came to the room to build Agnihotra fires to return the Australian girls to health. Yes, they were healed.

Later, the two healed Australian girls and I accompanied George Eggleston to another Sai Baba Ashram where he burned a fire to invite in Krishna, a high entity of India, to help with healing work. Afterward we went a short way to a place called Lady of Lourdes Grotto, a shrine to Mary, mother of the Christ. While we were there, she made her presence known to me and to one of the Australian girls. I realized she knew I had been worried about a young German man I had brought to her seven years ago for help. At that time he was skin and bones. Today, Mary gave me the image of the young German who was 'filled out' and wearing a coarse brown shirt and pants typical of someone working in agriculture.

Another time I was in India at the Ashram of Shirdi Baba where a woman from North Ireland was attending an Agnihotra fire in a copper, pyramid-shaped Agnihotra pot placed near a fire inside the Ashram of Shirdi Baba. A child about two or three years old started bouncing around and ignoring the fire in the pot that was inches from her. I was worried and finally I opened my mouth to say, "This child is in danger of being burned!" To my surprise, Shirdi Baba, who left the earth many years ago, spoke, "These are my children." He said it in such a way that I knew he wanted me to not criticize.

From Margaret:

It is understood that Sai Baba is the incarnation of Shirdi Baba who also is no longer in the third dimension. I never visited their Ashrams.

Today, May 3, 2015, Wesak Day, I ask Sai Baba, Where are you?, and he answers, *Right here.*

I tell him, dear Sai Baba, we are writing our chapter on the holy day of May 3 and healing. I am told it is the day when the Buddha returns to earth and the Christ appears in a high valley in the Himalayas. On the computer, we have been listening to your beautiful singing.

* Glossary: Sai Baba singing.

Do you have words for us today?

Sai Baba replies: Yes, right now I am here with you. Yes, I am here with everyone who is focused on peace and harmony for the planet. It is so very simple to be peaceful. Just wish the other fellow the same peace you want to enjoy. It should not be a struggle. I am here giving everyone blessings for this special day.

The Higher Worlds and the human worlds are very close today. The stairway is through the heart. Turn the mind chatter off. Go into peace. My love rains down on you as a soft spring shower.

The flowers grow, the trees bloom, and I send my love to humanity constantly.

Reflect to each the same love. Devotion to me is expressed in loving others, helping others, lifting the vibration of the planet. Care must be taken to honor all, from the smallest particle to the largest mountain. Rest in that understanding as you seek to join the high celebration of Wesak.

All life is a celebration. Be joyful. Be grateful. Be truly alive. I smile at my people. I send letters of love. Thought letters, songs, frequencies during this beautiful month of May.

Keep going. Keep smiling. Keep loving.

With love, Sai Baba

From Barbara:

After the channeling, Margaret and I feel we need to add more in this chapter about Sai Baba.

Devotees always love to visit Sai Baba and one of them was a British male married to a woman who was a devoted Christian. She agreed to accompany her husband to see Sai Baba but she was nervous because she felt a slight violation of her Christian belief.

Sai Baba invited the two to a private meeting, and while this was happening, the woman's camera started clicking. Sai Baba told her she would be surprised when she sees what has just been sent to her via the camera.

Guess what? The developed photograph is a picture of the Christ!

Sai Baba himself liked the Christ very much. He even had a small statue of the Christ in his garden.

One time I was visiting Sai Baba's Ashram and I had with me a copy of the Christ photograph from the lady's camera. I was seated on the grass when he walked by, and I put the photograph over my head. He paused and put his finger over the photograph and my head. It was only for an instant but I felt powerful Light.

Afterward, I took the photograph to the Ashram registration room that had a table with a glass top. Here, the photograph of the Christ was put under the glass so that all registering would see it. For those who may be nervous like the woman, they would feel reassurance.

As an aside, Sai Baba has a good sense of humor. One time I was asked to help break a serious drought. In meditation, I 'went there', flying over some clouds. Who was in the clouds? Sai Baba. He was with his broom sweeping in the clouds. I knew this was his humor for me. He told me it was not the proper time to break the drought. I needed to wait for the coming monsoon season. Oh!

I checked the Internet and realized I was a couple months ahead of the monsoon season. As a P.S., the monsoon stopped the drought! Much rain!

CHAPTER 11

THE FUJI DECLARATION

F rom Barbara:

As mentioned earlier in this book, May 17, at the foot of Mount Fuji, Japan, the Fuji Declaration would be inaugurated. Many would be gathered there as well as in Copenhagen, and in fact, throughout the world many would be observing the inauguration in their own communities.

What is The Fuji Declaration? An effort to awaken the Divine Spark in humanity so that love and peace and happiness can prevail.

Here is channeling from Saint Germain to Margaret:

Margaret, the earth is in a period of turmoil. Each country is facing its own political and environmental turmoil expressed in earthquakes, volcanoes, large storms, hurricanes, tornadoes. The people are very unsteady and agitated, reflecting the conditions on the planet. Which comes first – the peoples' agitation or the land's agitation? They are interchangeable.

Calm is needed. Balance is needed. Truth is needed. The gates between cultures need to be open and the moderate people need to communicate, exchange positive (love, light) frequencies for there to be peace and balance on the planet.

The Fuji Declaration takes the world agenda off focusing on religions to a more universal focus of cooperative human interaction based on the symbol of the mountain, Mount Fuji, which is balanced on all sides, soaring up to Heaven. The Nature world, Mount Fuji, is more stable than the human world. It is time for the perfection of Heaven to be reflected in perfection on earth.

The speaking now needs to be moderate, seeking harmony between people. Shocking confrontations create shockwaves that further destabilize the earth systems. The drumbeat of war, frequencies of conflict, need to be turned down and peace frequencies, harmonies, cooperation need to be emphasized.

The Fuji document seeks to do this – to counterbalance the turmoil of Earth at this time. Turn down the fire of rhetoric. Turn up the frequencies of peaceful co-existence. If the 'co' is taken out, then there will be no existence on the planet.

Peace is of upmost importance.

Saint Germain

From Barbara:

I think I mentioned earlier that Margaret and I had intended to go to Japan for the May 17 inauguration, but we cancelled because we were cautious about earth unrest and also we felt we should remain in North America to support from here the Declaration. However, we have added an interesting element to our participation. Yes, we will remain in North America, but we have joined with Carmen Balhestero of Sao Paulo, Brazil, to give a Fuji Declaration speech via SKYPE at the same time as the Japan ceremony. Carmen's Peace agency (PAX) will take our SKYPE message and broadcast it to the world via TV. Margaret and I will be speaking in English and Carmen will be translating into Portuguese.

* Glossary: Carmen Balhestero, Fraternidade PAX Universal, PAXTV.

Here is my talk that went out to the world:

Hello, everyone, this is Barbara Wolf from the United States. In our minds, we expand ourselves to be citizens of the entire world. We consider our work to be world work. Peace and Love, that is our world work.

I, Barbara, have a world organization, Global Meditations Network. People register from all over the world. When they register, they give their names only. They are not asked where they live, what they do, their age, their beliefs.

When an important message needs to be known to the world, I send the message to the Global Meditations Network so the members can send this message to their friends and family. If they are with a group, I know they will send the message to the group. Maybe there are 1,000 in the group. One click of the computer can connect the message to these 1,000 who will send out the message.

So you see what happens when one message is sent to the Global Meditations Network? This message spreads out and out and out until millions receive it.

Have you heard of the concept called the 100th monkey? One monkey learns how to wash sweet potatoes in a certain way. Other monkeys watch and they adopt the same method. When 100 monkeys are washing the sweet potatoes the same way, the concept is that all monkeys will wash them the same way.

When the Global Meditations Network sends out an important message, wouldn't the 100th monkey concept fit?

Today we are gathered here to speak about The Fuji Declaration. When the world becomes sufficiently aware, wouldn't the 100th monkey concept fit? Wouldn't the declaration be adopted world wide?

What is the intention of The Fuji Declaration? To awaken the divine spark in the spirit of humanity so that all of civilization on Mother Earth will act in peace and harmony.

This does not mean that everyone on Planet Earth must live the same way. Must comb their hair the same way. Must brush their teeth the same way. Must dress the same way. What is wanted is that everyone lives with the energies of peace and harmony and love. When help is needed, they will help each other.

Can you imagine how wonderful it would be if everyone on this planet woke every day with their hearts full of love?

As for myself, I think this would bring health to all. We would be singing the same healthy song of love. What has been within us that is not compatible will fly away.

For a moment, let us think of the birds when they sing. They are happy. For a moment, let us be like the birds singing with happiness.

The Fuji Declaration says it wants to awaken the divine spark in the spirit of humanity. The spark of love and happiness. In that way we will have a civilization of oneness. Yet, everyone can be different and that is acceptable. There will be much diversity on Mother Earth, but all will have the common concept of a heart full of love.

To me, the words "Awakening the Divine Spark" has to do with the heart of love. Today we all know harmony is on the edge of going down. We don't want that. We want all to hold hands with each other with love. We want the Divine Spark to be awakened.

And yes, when our Divine Spark is awakened, we need to look beyond ourselves and even beyond humanity. Nature is all around us. We need to look with love to the trees and the flowers and the birds and the animals. Also, to the structure of Mother Earth – the mountains, the rivers, her vast lands.

Can you imagine what this world would be like when negativity is turned off and the positive faucet is turned on to its fullest? If a misstep happens, we can step in immediately with Peace and Harmony.

The Fuji Declaration brings out the concept that individuals with diverse interests should work together so that all minds can have the experience of learning that diversity should not lead to misunderstandings. Scientists, artists, politicians, business leaders, etc. should work together to bring forth cooperation when helping to forge new ideas that will be harmonious for the world. This cooperation among diverse minds can bring forth a happy flourishing of life for all.

Coherent relations with all on this planet, including Nature, can bring about unity, and this unity will spread further out from this planet to embrace the cosmos and all beyond our Mother Earth. To understand the declaration concept, we are asked to consider that the organs and cells of our body must work together to maintain a healthy body so that we can use our body in harmony with all life everywhere.

Again, let us remember that on May 17, in Japan, there will be a formal inauguration ceremony of The Fuji Declaration, a call for a Divine Spark Activation that will radiate from Mount Fuji out to the world. The international community is asked to support this wonderful event. Let us remember the 100th monkey concept. We want The Fuji Declaration to succeed!

Now I want to end my talk so you may listen to a message from Mother Earth channeled by Margaret Anderson.

From Margaret:

Thank you for your work. I can feel the many people who care about spreading out the intensity of the pressure build up, relieving the pressure. Humanity needs to come together and be planetary focused. Earth problems would cease if humans become focused on the entire earth, i.e. not just one speck, one area, one region. View me from space. View yourself from space and then you will have the correct perspective. What was so large is not large anymore.

Love reigns. Love lasts. Love enhances all. Walk with love. Be love.
I am Love spreading Light through the Universe.

Gaia, Mother Earth.

From Barbara:

Before the Fuji Declaration May 17 event, Margaret and I realize we should work on three aspects to help make the Declaration strong -- the water, the land, the animals. Why do we need to make these three elements as strong as we can? Because, when people begin practicing the Declaration by sending out the good energies of Love, Peace, and Harmony, we want the result to be the best for all receivers, including water, land, and animals. Beforehand, we will 'coat' them with good energies.

First we will work with the water. We will go to Mendon Ponds, part of the Niagara Escarpment.

Margaret Channeling with Kirael of the 7th Dimension:

Dear Kirael, we are going to Mendon Ponds to place Nano Vita Water in the water for healing all the world waters. With our minds, we will see that it is done, that it has made a difference.

We will work with the Sun who gives love and energy to Mother Earth and the Moon who gives balance and vitality to all the waters of the planet. Can you advise what more we should do?

From Kirael:

Hello Lassie, Hello Lassies. Top of the morning to ye. The sweet day begins for healing Mother Earth. Send your love into her deep core, her heart. The planet has moved on but the residue of the injury remains.

Place the salve of love on her heart. The animals do this instinctively. The rocks abide and attend. Only humans dally into the folly of destructive practices that damage the physical being of the planet. What is sent out comes back. Make certain it is only love that is sent forth.

Continue with your work. You are needed.

Blessings and my love.

Your friend, Kirael

From Barbara and Margaret:

We begin driving to Mendon Ponds, the powerful eastern point of the Niagara Escarpment made over millions of years by accumulated sea life that lived and died during Mother Earth's period of positivity. The negative had not been introduced for humans to use. Since everything remains in consciousness, the Niagara Escarpment remains positive.

When we begin driving, the sky is cloudless, a bright blue. However, very soon clouds appear in the blue sky. We know these clouds disguise the presence of our brothers and sisters living in the galaxy. We say hello and continue driving to Mendon Ponds. As we turn into the park, we are ready to say hello to our frog friends living down the first hill in a patch of water. We always say hello to them.

And now we have a surprise. We see a chubby young woman sitting in a small ancient carriage driven by a small pony about the size of the carriage. The woman is aglow with joy and the pony seems to be joyfully trotting along pulling the little carriage.

We drive to our usual place of stopping in the park, close to the edge of a large pond. Now a big horse being ridden by a woman comes into view and a dog is trotting beside the horse. So, we have seen two horses in the park this morning. Two women interacting with the animal kingdom.

All about us is Nature. Trees not yet with leaves because the weather has been too 'Arctic' this spring. A daffodil or two has come out. Geese roosting here during our last journey are no longer evident.

Now it is time for us to begin our work. We leave the car and walk to the edge of the water. Margaret has in her hand a white cup into which she puts a bit of water. I take from my vest pocket a tiny bottle of Nano Vita Water given to me by Chinese Doctor Cua who practices ancient healing methods. I open the Nano Vita Water bottle and put some drops into the white cup with water in Margaret's hands. With the motion of an arch, she swishes water into the pond and we watch as this water retains the shape of an arch that becomes wider and wider in the pond water.

Overhead are our visitors from Outer Space. The sky is crowded with their cloud disguises. We know our space visitors are helping us to put our minds to spreading the Nano Vita Water from this pond to every speck of water on the planet.

It is our miracle. It is their miracle.

Because we know that water has a consciousness, with our minds, we can visualize that all water throughout the world has been given healing Nano Vita Water. Yes, we are cleaning the waters of Mother Earth. Our space visitors are helping.

Now we have one other big job to do here. We put more Nano Vita Water in the pond, and in that split second, we visualize we are cleaning the center of Mother Earth.

Later Kirael Channeling to Margaret:

Yes, you have made your way to the center chambers of Mother Earth's heart through your love and concern for the planet. You were helped by others, the higher energy of others from other homelands, to lift the energy of the Nano Vita Water thrown throughout the world, throughout space. Pure intent, Love. Mendon Ponds, a familiar vessel of purity and tranquility, is used to spread a frequency out on Mother Earth which is so needed because of the disruptions of the volcano fires and earthquake fracturing, jolting.

Walk in Peace. Go in Peace, Lassie, Lassies.

Your friend Kirael of the 7th Dimension

From Barbara:

We are satisfied with today's work with water to help Mother Earth. Tomorrow we will be working with the land, Letchworth State Park not far from us. But tonight, our thoughts are on Stonehenge. Why? We cannot answer this question.

We know the Higher Worlds have put Stonehenge into our minds.

We check the Internet and we find there is a reference to sound and Stonehenge. But I do not understand the work. The usual method is to create work from words put into our minds. The Internet says that different parts of Stonehenge have different tones when struck. Well, my mind is 'struck', but not well enough to understand what the Higher Worlds want us to do with the power of sound.

Margaret Channeling:

Dear Kirael, what is the meaning of Stonehenge in relationship to our work and the ancient Nature Kingdom?

Dear Lassie, slow down, slow down. You are too agitated to receive clarity of communication.

Stonehenge presents aspects according to the viewer. If the seeker seeks mystery, it is there. If the seeker seeks comfort, it is there. If the seeker seeks healing, it is there. If the seekers seek peace, it is there.

It is a sound resonator. It is a sound enhancer that goes out on different frequencies. If sent with love and healing frequencies, then the Vortex of Love and Healing is sent out. Use Stonehenge as a stamp, a vessel for holding a seal. It is a message carrier, an intersection of dimensions, an overlay. It can overlay the resonance of peace to augment positive energies.

Love and healing is the drama of the Vortex of Love. Stonehenge is the enactment of the Vortexes in stone. It amplifies anything of positive intent. May Peace Prevail On Earth. May Peace Prevail in all layers of Mother Earth, the aspects of the rock layer, the air current layers, vegetation, humanity, animals, sea creatures, angelic layers.

It is a lens. It is a soundboard. It is a record – the whales in stone who sing, who balance Mother Earth by their presence. The circle spirals Love and Peace. The circle is Light. Come walk amidst the circle.

The circle is an oasis of calm and of power. All people who approach must walk in dignity, in peace. This is the core essence.

With love, in truth, Kirael

From Barbara:

When we are ready to begin our drive to Letchworth State Park to work on the land, the sun is cooperating with us by shining brightly. This will not be a long drive, and we are delighted to return again to this 'Grand Canyon of the East' that has been miraculously spared the hand of man who likes to alter things. The land has sat a long, long time in peace and quiet.

Walking the land here is not easy. Viewing stops are accessed by road and the viewing is always spectacular. Can you image looking across at a deep 300 to 500 foot canyon of barren stone that was created millions of years ago? One can look across at this ancient site and see where an era begins and stays a very long time before rocks of a different configuration show a new era. Yes, it is wonderful to visit this very tranquil place that has not been beaten up by careless humanity. The trees have just begun to bud because this Northeast area of the continent has experienced a late spring.

At a lookout, we meditate and listen to the music, Let There Be Peace On Earth. I send the music, and especially the woman's voice to the center of the earth. At the same time, I send the music and her voice to Stonehenge so that mighty monument to Nature can send the SOUND out to all the surface of Mother Earth. Yes, it is delicious working here at 'the Grand Canyon of the East'. Stonehenge may be far away, but in meditation, it stands right beside me doing the work. I am happy I figured out why Stonehenge has been put into my mind in connection with my work.

It is tranquil here today. Very, very few people. Good. Easier to work for Mother Earth. We are reluctant to leave Letchworth State Park, but there is more work to be done and our thoughts now need to be turned to the animals. As a reminder, basically, we are helping to set up the 'tone' for May 17, the moment of The Fuji Declaration when a Divine Spark is to be awakened within humanity so that humanity can send Love and Peace and Harmony.

Yes, we are satisfied working with the 'tone' and Stonehenge has greatly helped.

As for a representative of the animal kingdom, we have decided to have the buffalo represent all the animals living on Mother Earth. We know there are many buffalo living in the countryside near a friend's house and quite quickly we have set up an arrangement with her to take us to the buffalo.

We choose a day that has beautiful sunshine and the trees are beginning to think about ending their rest for the winter. When we reach the countryside near our friend's house, we see orchards and orchards of apple trees ready to awaken. Good! Drinking cider, eating apples, hold our attention. We want a good crop this coming year.

Very soon, we are in the 'land of the buffalo'. There are many and they are roaming free. What a surprise! Yes, there are fences in this farming community, but somehow the buffalo know how to roam anyway. I think the fences are to keep them off the road so they will not be run over by careless drivers.

Hello! Hello! We see many buffalo! Maybe seventy seated on the ground in a vast clump. Sunbathing. I think they are sunbathing. There are trees just behind them, and I am thinking that these trees keep them cool during the summer because the trees will be blocking the sun. Well, today the buffalo are sunbathing and the trees are alone behind them.

Earlier, by telepathy, I have told the buffalo guardian that when we reach the buffalo today, we want two to come close enough to us so that we can exchange greetings telepathically. Well, here are 70 plus buffalo seated, sunbathing, and they are about 1,000 feet from us. Not close. Will two get up and start coming toward us? Well, one, a female, rises to her feet and begins walking slowly toward us. We sit in the car, parked, watching. Now a smaller buffalo gets to his feet and begins following her. The son, I am thinking.

The female increases her pace to a near trot. Behind her, the son begins to trot also, and then he trots faster and faster to catch up with her.

We are sitting in the car watching this drama. My feeling is that the Higher Worlds prompted her and her son to do this.

But now there is a hindrance. A farmhouse is between us and the two trotting buffalo, and a fence has been built. This will block our potential friends from coming close to us. Well, never mind. Hello, you two buffalo, we love you.

We wait for a few moments and then our friend begins driving us again. The land starts to drop so that after a short time we come to a large pond and stop. Before us, without exaggeration, three hundred plus white snow geese are clumped together in the water. They are not moving. They are not eating. They are roosting. My thought is that they have flown in from the South and they are resting until tomorrow when they will be flying north to their summer homeland.

And so, thank you, Higher Worlds, for providing us with this great flock of children from the sky of Mother Earth.

I am thinking of the animals and the birds and The Fuji Proclamation and my emotions border on tears.

Thank you, Higher Worlds.

From Margaret:

The next day, I channel the Buffalo:

Yesterday we had an amazing outing to see you, to tell you about the human effort to pray for peace and stability for Mother Earth on May 17, the high time of The Fuji Declaration.

It is wonderful seeing you resting on a small hill with the trees behind you. Your winter coats are dark, matching the ground and the tree bark. You are so peaceful sitting in the late morning sun on the south side of the hill. The day is cold but you seem so warm in a great cluster.

Dear Buffalo, can you comment on your thoughts during our visit?

The Buffalo respond: *We are grazing. We are resting. We are walking from place to place. The Earth is stable here and our movements are deliberate unless disturbed or agitated. It is the human factor that brings agitation. It is good that humans have an understanding to be and project calm and peace, to greet the movements of the sun and the moon. We prefer to be with our own where we are together, not disturbed by outside factors – cars, humans, dogs.*

We are solid in our being. We prefer to remain undisturbed. The basic essence of the Buffalo is strength and calm. We bring stability to where we are. The earth is our home. Mother Earth thrives where we roam. We give her stability, harmony, and she gives us rest and shelter and food. It is a sweet give and take. Our basic nature is stability. Let the humans learn from us. Admire us from a distance. Be calm and then your environment will be calm.

The Buffalo.

From Barbara:

The next day, we receive a message from the Higher Worlds to visit the zoo to intermingle with animals from all over the world. It is only a short drive to the Seneca Park Zoo. The sky is clear and the sun is bright. It is a bit chilly for the beginning of May, but Mother Earth is just now beginning to think about warm weather. Maybe she has a warm winter suit she likes to wear, a suit for comfort during freezing temperatures and she does not want to give it up.

When we arrive at the large zoo parking lot, we are surprised it is full of big school buses and cars. We know the buses mean a field trip for the students, but who is driving all these cars? Later, we learn they belong to the students' parents who want to visit the zoo with their offspring. In any case, there is room for our car.

When we enter the living quarters for the animals, Margaret stops to look at the snakes and I walk a few feet further to look at a bright orange long-haired tiny monkey no bigger than an oversized mouse. He is at the window when I approach the glass, and we face-to-face with each other. Then he becomes a bit bashful and he leaps to high branches where he can peek at me when he wants.

I walk a bit further to look at monkeys much bigger than the little one I have just left and they are friendly. Their shapes and sizes and colors are all different. One of them insists on walking high up in his cage by using a beam stretched about twenty feet from one side of the cage to the other side. He insists on walking upside down using the bottom of the wooden beam. I comment about this to a nearby zoo volunteer and she says I am looking at a two-toed sloth that likes to walk upside down.

Outside, we stop at a fenced-in enclosure for four male wolves, brothers, and here we speak with another zoo volunteer who tells us that all breeding at the zoo is well controlled. In fact the zoo is not allowed uncontrolled breeding. There has to be permission after all fertility information is known and this procedure, the volunteer says, applies to all at the zoo.

At the far end of the zoo, which has taken a bit of time to walk, there are four elephants, all female. Two Asian and two African. Their origin is immediately recognized by the ears. Big ears for African, smaller ears for other sources.

When we first arrive at the home of the four female elephants, we stand behind a fence and a pool of water. The four elephants are about a hundred feet from us eating bundled grass. One of them stops eating, turns toward us, and starts approaching to greet us. It is wonderful! At the same time, another elephant stops eating and goes inside enclosed living quarters.

When the elephant approaching us reaches the big pool, she stops and does not enter the water. We talk to her as we slowly move along the fence to the end of the pool, and then we walk along the fence until we reach a door to their indoor living quarters. When we open the door and walk in, we are greeted by a marvelous scene of an elephant being washed by zookeepers. She is lying on her side and they are scrubbing her. When the scrubbing is finished, a hose is used for rinsing. We are told that the elephants are washed daily and we know the elephant we are watching is very happy.

All in all, it is a pleasure being at the zoo with all the animals. We try to be mindful of why we are told to come. Animals, as well as everything else on this planet are dependent upon the attitude of humans. Let there be Peace on Earth, especially during the time of The Fuji Declaration!

Margaret Channeling:

Dear Emma, we are told to go to the zoo to greet and to give our love and protection to the animals of the world. We are greeted by the snakes, monkeys, rhino, wolves, eagle, crane, Arctic bears, lions, frogs, turtles, and elephants. We stay with them a long time. A great female elephant comes over to greet us. The lions are next to the fence. The wolves are close by and not roaming.

I feel an underlying heaviness, a seriousness. Are the animals feeling Mother Earth's shocks? There was a 7.3 earthquake in Nepal, and many earthquakes in Hakone, Japan, with steam coming out. Mauna Loa is showing an earthquake. There was even one near Vancouver Island. Are the animals feeling them? Can you comment why we have been told to visit the world animals?

Emma: *Margaret, all life is interconnected and the animals feel the disruption on Mother Earth. Earthquake vibration is hitting major continents. The animals are affected. They have sensitive receptors to each shock.*

Look today here at the zoo at the correct actions of the humans – children, teachers, volunteers – all focused with love on the animals. They greeted the animals with love, wonder, and respect.

You went to the snakes first for they are closest to Mother Earth's surface. You honored the turtle and her plates and the frogs and their music. The elephants are so sensitive, receiving impulses through their feet and ears. Large ones, small ones, all affected. Humans, animals are all affected by the great upheaval on Mother Earth. What seems distant is close up. The winds of change are agitated. The space ships (clouds) appeared above.

There has been great unity today. A loving blessing of all Mother Earth's species.

The day was very special, complex, and the enormity hard to grasp. Correct relationship. Clarity for the future. Stand tall and stay centered in love, not fear. Balance is needed now. Seriousness and Balance. All is one and one is all in these times of change.

I am here. I am with you.

Love, Emma.

From Barbara:

We have prepared Mother Earth and all who live on her for the May 17 Fuji Declaration celebration to concentrate on love, peace and harmony throughout the world. We are ready for the uniting of the spark within the heart. We have done our best.

CHAPTER 12

THE GREAT INVOCATION

From Barbara:

We want to end this book by telling you about The Great Invocation celebrated yearly on World Invocation Day at the full moon of Gemini. The date this year is June 2. Emphasis is on a sacred, ancient mantra.

Here is my version of this mantra. Others may say it differently.

From the point of Light within the Mind of God
Let light stream forth into the minds of men.
Let Light descend on Earth.

From the point of Love within the Heart of God
Let love stream forth into the hearts of men.
Let love descend on Earth.

From the center where the Will of God is known
Let purpose guide the wills of men.

Goodwill is foremost here and it is the third such spiritual festival within the last two months. Indeed, the full moon is considered essential here because of its potency during the sending out of positive energies such as goodwill.

In Chapter 10 we told you about the Wesak Festival at the full moon of Taurus and the Easter observance at the full moon of Aries. At the full moon of Gemini on the World Invocation Day, June 2, we will be speaking via SKYPE to Carmen Balhestero's PAX Center in Brazil and our talks will be put on PAX TV to be sent to the world.

Here is a part of my speech.

Hello from my heart, everyone, this is Barbara Wolf.
I greet you today with love.
Who are you? Who am I speaking to?
You are a Divine Being.
You have come from a spark, a Divine Spark.
You have all the Divine ingredients within you.
You can think good thoughts. You can think no good thoughts.
When you think good thoughts, you are sparking the spark.

Can you imagine how you would feel if your purpose is to put ten, twenty, fifty good thoughts together? Think of all the good energy you are feeling. All the good energy you are sending out. You would be building right relationships.

Goodwill. World Goodwill. That is a good taste. Can you imagine everyone tasting World Goodwill? We would be living in Paradise.

Peace, Love, and Light,
Barbara Wolf

Now it is time for Margaret to tell you her June 2 talk to PAX TV for the world.

From Margaret:

Barbara has created a powerful talk on The Great Invocation and I wonder how I should proceed. Then I receive images of The Great Invocation concept.

First, for the water, I see a Golden Triangle of Light for the dolphins to swim in to spread out to the oceans the energies of The Great Invocation.

For the land, I see the Barbury Crop Circle of three spinning circles in a triangular format. These circles represent Light, Love and Purpose of The Great Invocation. There is one circle at the bottom of the triangle opened to give out the Plan.

For the air, I think of the Vortex of Energy of the Nature Spirits on the island of Fiji. In 2004, Barbara and I visited the Orchid Garden to acknowledge the fairies and their work. We poured in Love and in return, they gave us immense Light in a great spinning Vortex.

As for fire, I think of Pele, the Goddess of Fire, who holds Love and Light and Power in her fire.

And so these are visual images of the message concept of The Great Invocation expressed on sea, land, air, and fire.

May each of us hold The Great Invocation in our hearts today to send out in our own way Light, Love and Purpose to restore the Plan on Earth.

Thank you. With love to all,
Margaret Anderson

Emma is asked if she has any words of wisdom about the times of now.

Her response:

Dear Margaret, it is a high time, it is a low time and it is your choice to pick the frequency. The key is what you send out. If you send out love, harmony and goodwill, then you will see the many acts of kindness around you. People are becoming more gracious and kind. The media delights in a diet of rancor, but the humans prefer to be calm, peaceful, centered and balanced.

Walk in the United Nations and you will see everyone concerned with peace, climate, food, gender issues, children's issues, etc. from all countries. These are what crosses all borders.

Strive daily to make the world a better place. Take the blinders off and see the reality of Nature. There is so much to learn and so much to share.

This is why it is so important that you send your book out on June 2, The Great Invocation Day.

As you travel, hold the Invocation prayer close to you to give strength when needed. It is like a peace power cable to recharge as needed. You tap in deep resources. As you saw the analogy of The Great Invocation as a great swimming pool, you can stay in the shallow end or jump into the deep end. That is life.

Let the Plan of Love and Light work out.

My blessings to you and to your dear readers.

With love,
Emma

An observance from Barbara:

It is interesting that The Great Invocation has caught the attention of the United Nations. After all, that world institution started its roots with the intention of planting a better quality of life for many. And so, even though the United Nations is far from perfect, yet, the intention of giving out, giving out goodwill, remains.

And now it is time to end this book. The date today is June 2, 2015. We will hand over our manuscript to the publisher.

Goodbye, folks, it has been fun writing you.

Barbara and Margaret

_____

GLOSSARY

SACRED MUSIC

Musical Rapture, A Healing Gift for Humanity, can be downloaded free via Patricia Cota-Robles' website
http://www.eraofpeace.org/musical-rapture

As her son Joao stated on his mother's website: "The frequency of this Celestial Music communicates with the Divine Intelligence of the body at a cellular level raising the consciousness of each cell. As the music soothes and comforts the cells, the body's natural ability to heal itself is enhanced."

Paneurhythmy - The Dance of Life
https://www.youtube.com/watch?v=ygu0CHDhJOM

Australian Aboriginal Music: Song with Didgeridoo
https://www.youtube.com/watch?v=dFGvNxBqYFI

Michiko Moroi, Let There Be Peace On Earth In North America
https://www.youtube.com/watch?v=ZWCYrJoJe14

Sai Baba Singing
https://www.youtube.com/watch?v=HbEI2xq9OEw

HEALING

Emma Kunz, former artist, healer
http://www.emma-kunz.com/english/emma-kunz/

Dr. Luke Cua, Doctor of Chinese Medicine
http://newvita.com/education an http://newvita.com#

Agnihotra Information
http://www.agnihotra.org

OTHER

Carmen Balhestero PAX Center and PAXTV
http://pax.org.br and http://paxtv.com.br

The Fuji Declaration
http://fujideclaration.org

Ben Davidson, Recent Breakthroughs Reveal Startling Possibility: Water is Everywhere
http://wavechronicle.com/wave/?p=1151

Video, Total Solar Eclipse, March 20, 2015 - Spitsbergen, Arctic
https://vimeo.com/122795016

VORTEXES

Chief Golden Light Eagle and Grandmother SilverStar have given us valuable information on how to use powerful energy fields to help Mother Earth and all that live on her. This information has come from sacred ceremony and the information is available through:

1. New Title: The Symbols. The Universal Symbols and Laws of Creation: *A Divine Plan by Which One Can Live*, The Heavenly Hosts, The Servants of Creator. Copyright 1996 by Standing Elk.

2. The Vortexes, The Universal Symbols and Laws of Creation; *A Divine Plan by which One Can Live*, The Heavenly Hosts, The servants of Creation, Copyright 2013, Revised Edition. All Rights Reserved.

3. The EarthStar Way Calendar, A Sacred Cosmic Earth Moon Sun MorningStar Dance with The Seven Stars. The Universal Symbols and Laws of Creation in Day By Day Living. Copyright 1999-2016. All Rights Reserved.

To order:
http://www.starelders.net or http://www.starelders.net/store.htm

VORTEX LISTING

Two Star Law Symbols combined make one Vortex.

The **Vortex of Light, Sound and Vibration** is formed by joining the Symbol of the *Universal Law of Light, Sound and Vibration* with the Symbol of *Spiritual Law of Intuition*.

The **Vortex of Integrity** is formed by the *Universal Law of Free Will* combining with the *Spiritual Freedom of Man*. This is a free will planet and can only operate fully when there is complete spiritual freedom of man. There should be freedom with truth and honesty.

The **Vortex of Symmetry** is formed by combining the *Universal Law of Symmetry* with the *Spiritual Law of Equality*. Symmetry means balance between all things, both spiritual and material. As above, so below. Also, equality between male/female, left/right brain, etc.

The **Vortex of Strength, Health and Happiness** is formed with the combining of the *Universal Law of Movement and Balance* with the *Spiritual Strength, Health and Happiness*. In life one has to be balanced to move forward and also one has to move forward to be balanced. Balance is symmetry in motion. With movement and balance come strength and health and happiness.

The **Vortex of Right Relationship** is produced by combining the *Universal Law of Innocence, Truth and Family* with *Spiritual Protection of Family*. This is also a powerful Vortex of social relationship (based on truth) when the concept has moved from the individual to the group.

The **Vortex of Growth** is formed when the *Universal Law of Change* is combined with the *Spiritual Growth of Man*. Change is a basic tenant of life. With spiritual growth, all things thrive. All things change. Nothing is static. Therefore, both the individual and society need the spiritual growth of man. When humanity grows spiritually, then the Vortex of Growth flourishes. In the natural state, all things grow unhindered. With spiritual growth all things thrive.

The **Vortex of True Judgment** is formed by combining the *Universal Law of Judgment* with the *Spiritual Law of Karma*. All actions should be looked at through the eyes of the *Universal Law of Judgment* so that no harm is done and there is no karma. The latter, the consequences of action, can be turned into dharma, teaching. This law applies socially as well as environmentally.

The **Vortex of Perception** is formed by the combining of the *Universal Law of Perception* combined with the *Spiritual Law of Future Sight*. It is important to perceive the impact of one's actions and to use the gift of future sight. Needed now are planetary actions that affect in a good way the lives of the people in relationship to the air, the water, the land, the life on this planet.

The **Vortex of Connection to Life** is formed with the combining of the *Universal Law of Life* with the *Spiritual Law of Choice*. Life is enhanced by correct choices. It is diminished by poor choices. Therefore, choose wisely. Choice and Life are integrally connected.

The **Vortex of True Nature** is formed by the combining of the *Universal Law of Nature* with the *Spiritual Law of Protection*. Nature exists and thrives. It is up to mankind to protect Nature so that all life thrives on this planet.

The **Vortex of Love** is formed by combining the *Universal Law of Love* with the *Spiritual Law of Healing*. One has to have Love to give healing and to receive healing. Love is the greatest healer. People, Nature, all creatures, plants, cells, molecules, atoms, adamantine particles respond to Love. All have a consciousness. Love creates. Love heals. Love is the highest power of all.

When the Vortexes are displayed in a circle, the center point, a Vortex forms and is called **Universal Unity and Spiritual Integrity**. All Vortexes bring unity. All Vortexes thrive with integrity. Integrity is the foundation of the Vortexes.

Printed in the United States
By Bookmasters